D1157669

FIELD GUIDE TO

BACKYARD BIRDS OF THE

SOUTH

Published by Cool Springs Press
A Waynick Book Group Company
101 Forrest Crossing Boulevard
Suite 100
Franklin, Tennessee 37064
(615) 277–5555

ISBN-13: 978-1-59186-006-8

First Printing 2008
Printed in the United States of America
10 9 8 7 6

Project Manager: Ashley Hubert
Art Director: Marc Pewitt
Production: Publication Services, Inc.
Illustrator: Publication Services, Inc.

Photographs of the American Tree Sparrow and American Woodcock courtesy of Jupiter Images. All other photographs provided by Brian E. Small.

FIELD GUIDE TO
BACKYARD BIRDS OF THE
SOUTH

COOL
SPRINGS
PRESS

FRANKLIN, TENNESSEE

CONTENTS

INTRODUCTION

The warm, wet climate of the South provides a winter haven for hundreds of bird species that breed in the northern states or Canada. Every autumn mixed flocks select their winter habitats in deciduous forests, grasslands, everglades, or along sandy shores, where they enjoy a steady supply of insects and berries.

The region has an abundance of resident species as well. The northern mockingbird and Carolina wren sing cheerily in backyards along the Smoky Mountains, while colorful warblers abound in the vast pine-oak forests further south. Birders rarely experience a moment of silence in the cypress swamps of the South, where a steady chorus of bird calls is punctuated by the hammering of woodpeckers and the occasional splash as a belted kingfisher plucks a slippery silver fish from the murky water.

If you are new to birding, a few basic strategies will increase the likelihood of spotting and identifying local species. The first step is to obtain at least one useful field guide. Carry it with you in the field, and keep it on hand for easy use. When you sight an unfamiliar bird, watch its behavior, note its coloring and unique field marks, and then consult your guide to confirm its name.

The second item to keep handy near your observation window is a pair of binoculars. A quality pair can often be purchased for under $100, and 7x or 8x magnification is ideal.

Learning to recognize bird songs is another valuable investment. Audio CDs and online resources provide samples of hundreds of common bird calls and songs, and knowing the sounds of your common backyard residents will make it easier to recognize an uncommon visitor.

Consider joining a local birding club. These organizations frequently organize birding walks and field trips, where more experienced birders can answer your questions, help you identify unfamiliar species, and recommend the best local bird-watching sites.

The simplest way to begin birding is to watch the birds in your own backyard. Even a small yard with one or two feeders can be home to dozens of birds. Some affordable options for seed-eaters include black-oil sunflower seeds, white millet, peanuts, mixed seed, cracked corn, and thistle seed. Insectivores may be happily at home among garden trees and shrubbery, but in winter, many turn

Northern Mockingbird

to berries and suet cakes. Still others—hummingbirds, for example—are drawn to flowering plants.

Learning the dietary preferences of your favorite species can help you decide how best to draw them to your property. Bird boxes for cavity-nesting species are another easy way to intimately observe their behavior. Whether you encounter feathered friends close to home or far afield, birding is sure to become an exciting and rewarding hobby.

red

nesting sites and food in cities, towns, and farming areas.

Feeding Habits
Finches are common visitors to backyard seed feeding stations, and otherwise survive on fruit, bread crumbs, berries, buds, and flower parts.

Migration Habits
The introduced eastern population has thrived and spread across the continent, now separated from the native western population by less than 100 miles.

Placement of Feeders
While these welcome visitors are perched on your mixed seed feeder, try to distinguish the female house finch from the female house sparrow. Also, watch for finch nests in your hanging flower baskets or ornamental garden trees.

I n 1940 New York City pet shops began to sell California's native house finches as pet songbirds. In the ensuing crackdown on this practice, a small population of the brightly plumed birds was released. For years they straggled on Long Island, but eventually spread to suburban communities throughout the East.

Description
Similar to the purple finch of the North and West, the 6-inch male is brown above with a red brow, bib, and rump. The female, identified by a white eyebrow, and juvenile are paler with streaked bellies.

Preferred Habitat
Now widespread and common in both the East and the West, the house finch competes with the house sparrow for

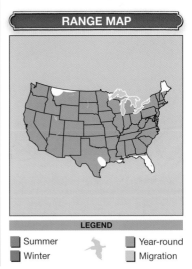

RANGE MAP

LEGEND

■ Summer	■ Year-round
■ Winter	■ Migration

U nusual among birds, cardinals mate for life and stay paired year-round. The colorful pair sings in duets, completing each other's loud whistled phrases *what cheer, cheer, cheer* or *sweet-sweet-sweet-sweet*. The male may act aggressively toward the female at a feeding station, but she continues feeding, undisturbed.

Description

Named for the robes of Catholic cardinals, the male's bright red plumage and black face are unmistakable. Females are grayish brown with red highlights on the crest, wings, and tail, and an orange-red bill. Both measure 7.5–9 inches long.

Preferred Habitat

Common in gardens, parks, thickets, woodlands, and hedgerows, cardinals nest in a shrub or a tangle of vines.

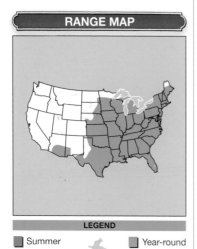

RANGE MAP

LEGEND

- ■ Summer
- ■ Winter
- ■ Year-round
- ■ Migration

Males feed the first brood while the female starts a second, with up to four broods each year.

Feeding Habits

Cardinals have a varied diet encompassing weed seeds, wild fruit, insects, grains, and even maple syrup from woodpecker holes.

Migration Habits

These nonmigrants are less territorial in winter, joining with small flocks. In recent decades their range has extended farther north.

Placement of Feeders

This frequent feeder visitor uses its short, conical bill to crack open seeds, especially sunflower seeds, safflower seeds, and cracked corn.

red

A bristly layer of feathers protects the nostrils from wood dust as the woodpecker hammers out a rapid message on a utility pole. This sturdy bird is equipped for a lifetime of climbing and drilling, bracing itself upright with a stiff tail and using its long toes to grip its perch.

Description

The 10-inch woodpecker is stout and strong, ladder-barred black and white above with a tan face and underparts. Males have a characteristic red crown and nape, while females have a red nape only.

Preferred Habitat

Any orchard, park, farmland, or open swampy woodland with a handful of dead trees might be home to the red-bellied, which bores a nest hole in dead tree trunks or utility poles.

Feeding Habits

Its stiff bill chips away bark to find insects, wood-boring beetles, seeds, and wild fruits. Its long, cylindrical tongue has a hard tip to spear insects and a sticky coating to lap up ants.

Migration Habits

Found in The South, the more northern birds may migrate further south in winter, where they are common in parks and southeastern woodlands.

Placement of Feeders

Listen for the woodpecker's low, hoarse rattling call. In winter they turn to feeders, and those wintering in Florida suck juice from oranges.

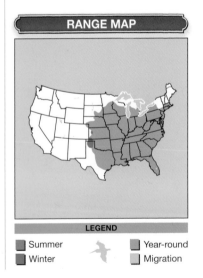

RANGE MAP

LEGEND

- Summer
- Winter
- Year-round
- Migration

Red-winged Blackbird

From his perch on a swaying cattail, the male blackbird sings his gurgled song while flashing his red shoulder patches, eagerly establishing his mating territory before the females arrive.

Description
This large blackbird, 7–9.5 inches, is common and unmistakable. The black male has bright red patches on shoulders bordered by a yellow band. Females and juveniles are heavily streaked with brown and lack the red patches.

Preferred Habitat
Perhaps most common in marshes, swamps, and wet meadows, this marsh bird will nest near any body of water, including dry pastures, farmland, and roadside ditches. Breeding birds construct a new nest of marsh reeds for each of the season's two or three broods.

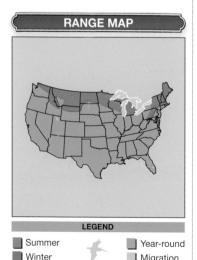

RANGE MAP

LEGEND

- Summer
- Winter
- Year-round
- Migration

Feeding Habits
Seeds provide the blackbird's main sustenance in spring and autumn, but it switches to insects for the summer season.

Migration Habits
Their extensive breeding range stretches from Alaska across Canada and the United States, and the birds winter across most of the United States, north to Washington, Michigan, and Pennsylvania.

Placement of Feeders
The flashy red-wing is a familiar sight in backyards and parks across the country, particularly when they join up with other blackbirds for autumn and winter feeding in mobs of hundreds of thousands or even millions.

Ruby-crowned Kinglet

red

Feeding Habits
Flicking its wings nervously in typical kinglet fashion, the bird bounds from branch to branch snatching aphids, spiders, and berries.

Migration Habits
Forests across much of the west are the kinglet's home in summer, and it is often glimpsed singing its surprisingly loud triplet song during migration. They winter across much of the southern half of the United States and West Coast, but can be found year-round in the far northwest.

Placement of Feeders
Kinglets join up with mixed flocks of chickadees and warblers for winter foraging. Watch for a tiny bird fluttering around a thick shrub near the ground.

Small as a hummingbird and drably attired, the ruby-crowned kinglet is easily overlooked most of the year. But during spring mating, chattering males raise a concealed crown of red crest feathers—a "flash patch"—to challenge other males.

Description
The tiny, olive-green kinglet is whitish below with two white wing bars, a white eye ring, and a solid olive face. The male's red crown patch is usually hidden.

Preferred Habitat
Tiny nests constructed of moss and spider webs and decorated with lichen hang from twigs in a tall conifer. Coniferous forests are ideal for breeding, but they spread to mixed forests and thickets in winter.

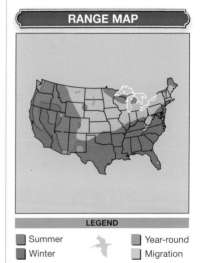

RANGE MAP

LEGEND

Summer — Year-round

Winter — Migration

Despite its bright, tropical appearance, the 7-inch tanager can be tough to spot in the forest canopy. The Tupi tribe in South America assigned the name "tanager," meaning a small, brightly colored bird.

Description

Breeding males have black wings against vivid red bodies. Females and juveniles are yellow-green above with olive wings and tail. In autumn, males molt their scarlet plumage and look like the female.

Preferred Habitat

These tanagers occasionally reside in parks and gardens, but they prefer mature deciduous or mixed oak forests to nest, requiring approximately 4–8 acres per nesting pair. The female builds a flimsy platform nest of twigs

red

and leaves on a horizontal branch of a deciduous tree.

Feeding Habits

Hovering high in the tree canopy, the tanager plucks insects, spiders, fleshy fruit, and flower buds from foliage.

Migration Habits

After a long migration from Central and South America, small flocks of tanagers arrive at their summering grounds in late spring. They breed east of the Great Plains, from Minnesota to New England and south to Georgia.

Placement of Feeders

Although elusive, the tanager may be lured to a feeding station high above the ground offering fresh oranges or a peanut butter and suet mix.

RANGE MAP

LEGEND

■ Summer ■ Year-round
■ Winter ☐ Migration

This master of disguise is so well camouflaged that birders may walk right past without noticing him. Sitting silently with its bill turned straight up to the sky, the bittern can take on the appearance of a tree stump, a root, or a dead limb, or it can sway back and forth to blend in perfectly with its reedy home.

Description

The pear-shaped bittern ranges from 24–34 inches long, streaked dark brown above, with dark wingtips and yellow legs and feet. Its white throat has long, reddish brown stripes.

Preferred Habitat

In secretive, isolated pairs the bitterns build a reed platform nest near the water's edge in marshes, fens, grassy lakeshores, large wetlands, or wet meadows.

Feeding Habits

Standing in the shallow water, the bittern waits in perfect stillness until a hapless fish draws near, then it plunges its stiff beak into the water to stab its meal. Insects, frogs, crayfish, reptiles, eels, and water snakes are common prey.

Migration Habits

This water-loving bird migrates throughout the central and southern United States. It can be found wintering along the southeastern coast.

Placement of Feeders

In March and April, the usually solitary, silent males make brief public courtship displays. Between dusk and midnight, listen for a low-pitched *oonk-a-lunk* call.

RANGE MAP

LEGEND
Summer   Year-round
Winter   Migration

brown

This small bird, only 10 inches long, makes an incredible journey each spring and autumn of nearly 10,000 miles over the Atlantic between Canada and South America, or over the Pacific to Australia for its well-deserved winter rest.

Description
Spring adults are mottled black flecked with gold above and below, with a white S-shaped stripe from the crown to the shoulders. By autumn they molt into whitish underparts, with less gold above and a paler eyebrow.

Preferred Habitat
During spring migration the birds rest in agricultural fields on their way to their breeding grounds in the tundra of northern Canada and Alaska. During autumn migration they prefer mud flats

and sod farms.

Feeding Habits
Plovers consume mainly insects, mollusks, and crustaceans, but often fatten up on crowberries before their long journey.

Migration Habits
Flocks of 500 to 5,000 pass through the central United States during spring migration from South America to the far North. In autumn, much smaller flocks cruise along the coast of the Atlantic.

Placement of Feeders
Watch for tired birds riding the winds or resting in wet crop fields during migration periods. Plovers were once hunted in huge numbers, but they are now federally protected and their populations are bouncing back.

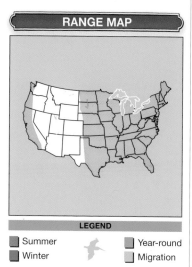

RANGE MAP

LEGEND
- Summer
- Winter
- Year-round
- Migration

During spring courtship, the male woodcock gives a fascinating display. After sunset, and sometimes all night long, he parades around his territory buzzing like an insect, then leaps into flight crooning a warbling song, then dives in zigzags back to the ground.

Description

Stocky and large-headed, the 11.5-inch woodcock is mottled brown with a camouflage leaf pattern above and rust or buff below. The bill is very long, and the eyes are set far back beneath a black-barred crown.

Preferred Habitat

Woodcocks raise their broods in brushy fields, moist thickets, or damp woodlands. After breeding season, they relocate to marshes, wetlands, and swamps.

Feeding Habits

In 24 hours a woodcock can eat its weight in earthworms, plucking them out of the loose earth with its long bill. They also consume insects, berries, and the seeds of some grasses and weeds.

Migration Habits

You will find the woodcock year-round in most of The South. They are found in the East and the Midwest, breeding in the North and wintering along the Gulf of Mexico.

Placement of Feeders

From mid-March to June, but especially in April, listen for the male's sensational courting song, or their common *peent* call.

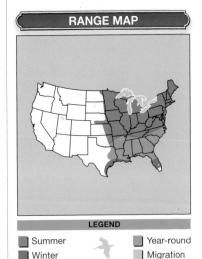

RANGE MAP

LEGEND

Summer   Year-round
Winter   Migration

This plain-looking bird is a remarkable songster, gracing the ears with a beautiful caroling medley. When undisturbed, the sparrow issues a long, elaborate song from a high perch. However, they are elusive in winter.

Description
Measuring 5.75 inches, the reddish-brown sparrow is heavily streaked above and on the crown and plain buff below, with a rusty stripe through the eye.

Preferred Habitat
Open pine or oak forest is the best place to spot these sparrows, though they also inhabit brushy pastures and palmettos in The South. Their domed nest of grass, entered from the side, is concealed beneath a grassy clump or shrub. Weather permitting, the sparrows sometimes raise two broods a season.

RANGE MAP

LEGEND
- Summer
- Winter
- Year-round
- Migration

Feeding Habits
Bachman's sparrow eats mainly insects and spiders, available year-round in its southern habitat, as well as seeds.

Migration Habits
This sparrow resides primarily in the Southeast, summering north and wintering from Louisiana to North Carolina.

Placement of Feeders
Follow its flowing song with your binoculars to scan the forest canopy for a small red-brown bird. You will be rewarded with the sight of a male in rapturous song, head thrown back and chest booming.

brown

wooden nest box, or in an abandoned hawk's nest.

Feeding Habits
Although primarily nocturnal, the barred species is often seen hunting during daylight, seeking mice, frogs, snakes, insects, rodents, small owls or birds, and crayfish.

Migration Habits
Owls are common year-round in the South and along the Pacific Coast to California.

Placement of Feeders
On overcast afternoons, their unique calls can lead you straight to their roosts, where they are calm and tame. Also try imitating their simpler calls to lure them near.

I n the resounding darkness of the deep woods at night, a chilling call rings out—*Who cooks for-you, who cooks for you-all?* The nocturnal barred owl is a varied vocalist, with calls that include hoots, howls, barks, and squawks.

Description
At 18–24 inches, this squat owl is twice the size of the Eastern screech-owl, and females are slightly larger. Its ruffled plumage is brown above and pale below, with dark horizontal barring across its chest, vertical streaks on the belly, and white barring down its back.

Preferred Habitat
In dense woodlands, river valleys, or swamps, females lay eggs on the bare floor of a tree cavity, in a simple

RANGE MAP

LEGEND

■ Summer   ■ Year-round
■ Winter   ▢ Migration

This warbler's population fluctuates in relation to cyclical infestations of spruce budworms, pests that devastate spruce forests. In infestation years, there may be up to six times as many bay-breasted warblers.

Description
Measuring 5-6 inches long, breeding males have chestnut on the crown, throat, and sides, with a black face and forehead, a pale ear patch and buff underparts. Females are similar but lack the side patches. Nonbreeding males are dull green with buff sides.

Preferred Habitat
In spruce forests across Canada, the bird builds a bulky cup of twigs, bark, and grass in a conifer. During budworm years, females lay two additional eggs.

brown

Feeding Habits
To minimize competition with other warblers, this bird scours mid-level branches for caterpillars, spiders, flies, budworms, and insect larvae. In their wintering grounds in South America, they eat mostly fruit.

Migration Habits
In summer they are found in parts of Minnesota and New England. In winter they cross The South on their way to Panama and Colombia.

Placement of Feeders
Watch for this common migrant from May to June, when they are easy to identify, but once they drop their breeding plumage, males look very similar to blackpoll warblers.

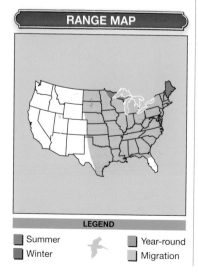

RANGE MAP

LEGEND
- Summer
- Winter
- Year-round
- Migration

brown

The elusive brown thrasher is most likely to be glimpsed in spring, when, from its perch on a sapling, it initiates elaborate courting rituals characterized by eloquent, rapturous song. Closely related to the mockingbird, the thrasher can mimic more than 1,100 songs, usually sung in couplets with each phrase repeated twice.

Description
Though similar in appearance to a thrush, the thrasher is larger, streaked rather than spotted, with a longer tail. Measuring 10–12 inches, this thin bird is rusty brown with white wing bars and whitish, brown-streaked underparts.

Preferred Habitat
Brushy woodlands, garden shrubbery, and parks provide protection for this shy bird, which has recently become scarce for unknown reasons.

Feeding Habits
Foraging on the ground, the thrasher scares up insects, spiders, and berries.

Migration Habits
A resident of the Southeast year-round, the thrasher arrives in the Northeast and Midwest to breed in mid to late April.

Placement of Feeders
This shy bird prefers to forage on the ground within the safety of a thorny or shrubby den, and will stop singing or flee when it realizes it's being observed. They may nest in yards with sufficient cover, and visit feeders for scratch feed, millet, suet, or raisins.

RANGE MAP

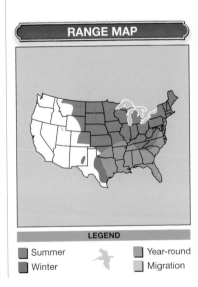

LEGEND

Summer   Year-round
Winter   Migration

Just before dawn, while a female songbird is away from her nest, an intruder rolls an egg out of the nest and replaces it with her own. The imposter fledgling will dominate the other chicks until it grows to maturity and rejoins its original species, the brown-headed cowbird. Often vilified as a brood parasite, the female cowbird leaves more than 20 eggs each season in the nests of more than 200 other species.

Description

The 6–8 inch glossy black male has a brown head, while the female is grayish brown overall. Both issue a *check* or rattling call.

Preferred Habitat

Once found only in the Great Plains, where it followed roaming buffalo

herds, the brown-headed cowbird has thrived on suburbanization and is today found from coast to coast, favoring woodland edges, thickets, roadsides, and towns.

Feeding Habits

Alongside other blackbirds and starlings, the cowbird forages on the ground for insects, seeds, and grains. Grasshoppers are a particular favorite.

Migration Habits

With its summers spent in the West, the cowbird can be found year-round in The South.

Placement of Feeders

This bird is drawn to grains, seeds, berries, cracked corn, or sunflower hearts.

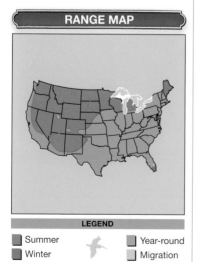

RANGE MAP

LEGEND

- Summer
- Winter
- Year-round
- Migration

brown

Feeding Habits
Flitting from plant to plant, these omnivores eat primarily insects and other small animals, as well as fruit and seeds.

Migration Habits
Carolina wrens inhabit the South and Midwest year-round, never migrating, which means that a harsh winter can devastate populations. But young birds seem to expand northward after mild winters. They mate long term, staying paired year-round.

Placement of Feeders
As the only wren to frequent garden feeders, these cheery singers are drawn to fruit and suet, peanut butter, sunflower seeds, and nuts. They will often nest in birdhouses or other man-made objects, such as baskets, mailboxes, stone walls, or tin cans.

Switching without pause from *wheat-eater, wheat-eater, wheat!* to *tweedle, tweedle* or *tea kettle, tea kettle*, the Carolina wren sings up to 40 different songs all day long, regardless of season.

Description
Although similar to the house wren, the Carolina wren can be identified by its upturned tail. Measuring 6 inches, the bird is mainly reddish-brown with a white eyebrow swash, white chin, and buff underparts.

Preferred Habitat
Found in woodlands, thickets, undergrowth near water, and garden shrubs, the wren constructs small nests of grass, stems, and bark in a tree cavity or man-made object.

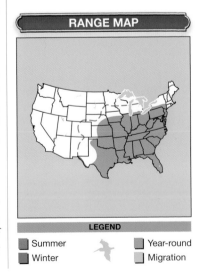

RANGE MAP

LEGEND

Summer Year-round

Winter Migration

Cedar Waxwing

These sleek, elegant birds are highly social, often seen lined up on a wire or branch passing berries or flower petals from one bird to the next. Best identified by a narrow, black "bandit" mask across the eyes, the crested bird has yellow tail tips and waxy red tips on the inner wing feathers.

Description
The 8-inch waxwing's plumage is a beautiful blend of soft pastel browns and grays above and below.

Preferred Habitat
Waxwings enjoy the close company of their own kind, making them one of the few songbirds to nest in colonies. They build bulky twig nests in open woodlands, orchards, gardens, and parks.

brown

Feeding Habits
The bird consumes mainly berries and flower buds from berry-bearing trees and shrubs, especially cedar cones. Overripe, fermenting berries cause temporary intoxication, a startling sight for observant birders. During summer they also catch insects.

Migration Habits
This stunning species breeds across the northern half of the United States wintering in the lower United States from the East Coast to the West Coast.

Placement of Feeders
Announcing their arrival with a high-pitched whistling, small winter flocks frequently descend on parks and gardens in search of cedar and rowan berries.

RANGE MAP

LEGEND

- Summer
- Winter
- Year-round
- Migration

brown

Long ago abandoning its traditional habitat, the chimney swift selected the hollow towers accompanying human settlements for its home, both in nesting season and during migration. At sundown swarms of these fast flyers funnel like a tornado into large chimneys.

Description
Shaped like a boomerang in flight, the 5.5-inch swift is one of the world's fastest flying birds. Adult birds are dark gray-brown all over, with a short, stubby tail and long, narrow, curved wings.

Preferred Habitat
This species is found in all habitats across the East. Adults use saliva to glue a twig nest onto a vertical wall within a chimney, barn, well, or tree cavity. A second male often assists with raising the fledglings.

Feeding Habits
The swift spends its life on the wing, swallowing insects whole as it flies and dipping into rivers and streams to drink and bathe.

Migration Habits
These birds breed from the Great Plains east to the coast, traveling to South America in September.

Placement of Feeders
Large flocks return to favorite chimney sites year after year. In place of suitable chimneys, specially designed towers can be erected to draw flocks to your own property.

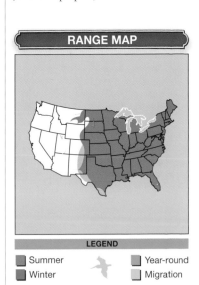

RANGE MAP

LEGEND

Summer

Winter

Year-round

Migration

A bandoning its ground foraging for the moment, a male chipping sparrow mounts a high perch to utter its rapid, monotonous trill, often likened to the sound of a sewing machine.

Description

Six-inch adults are brown streaked with black above and gray on the rump, sides, and underparts. Look for its chestnut crown, white eyebrow, and black line through the eye.

Preferred Habitat

Often found in backyard shrubs or evergreens, the bird thrives in farmland, orchards, open woodlands, and residential areas. High in a tree, the female lines a cup nest with hair plucked from a horse or dog to insulate the season's two broods.

Feeding Habits

In summer the chippy eats primarily insects, including spiders, caterpillars, wasps, weevils, grasshoppers, and other agricultural pests. In autumn small flocks forage on lawns for grass and weeds, surviving on seeds in winter.

Migration Habits

Notable as the most common migrant sparrow in North America, this bird has a long breeding season throughout most of the United States, wintering along the Gulf Coast into the Desert Southwest.

Placement of Feeders

Any birder with access to a developed backyard garden is sure to enjoy the presence of the domesticated chippy as it scours the ground beneath feeding stations.

RANGE MAP

LEGEND

- Summer
- Winter
- Year-round
- Migration

brown

Dickcissel

O nce residing only in midwestern grasslands, this species established a new breeding population in New England in the nineteenth century, which mysteriously disappeared, but simultaneously expanded its range across the Midwest. These fluctuations continue, as local populations are unpredictable from year to year.

Description
From a visible perch, the vibrant bird issues an incessant hissing or buzzing *dick-dick-cissel* song. The 7-inch breeding male, streaked brown above with a yellow breast, black bib, and chestnut wing patch, is easy to spot. Females and males in winter have a duller wing patch and no bib.

Preferred Habitat
Croplands, hayfields, and pastures provide a ready supply of food and safe ground nesting sites for the polygamous dickcissel's two annual broods.

Feeding Habits
Seeds and grain gathered from crops are staples, but insects gleaned from grassy fields are a favorite as well.

Migration Habits
Demonstrating an impressive traveling range, most dickcissels fly south to wintering grounds in Venezuela and return annually. You will see them spending their summers in the South.

Placement of Feeders
Although few of these sparrow-like birds will visit seed feeders in winter, those who do will be regulars.

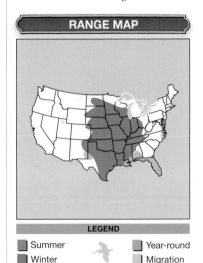

RANGE MAP

LEGEND

■ Summer
■ Winter
■ Year-round
■ Migration

Originally named "dunlings," meaning little dun-coloreds, these small, plump sandpipers measure only 6–8 inches.

Description
Breeding adults are reddish above and white below, with a large black patch on the belly. Winter adults are grayish brown above and whitish below. The best field mark is their long, black, downward-curving bill.

Preferred Habitat
The male reaches breeding grounds in Arctic or subalpine tundra in early June and awaits his devoted mate's arrival. Together, they build a ground nest, sharing incubation and feeding the chicks. During migration and winter, dunlins can be found on mud flats, and on beaches along ponds, lakes, or oceans.

RANGE MAP

LEGEND

Summer
Winter
Year-round
Migration

Feeding Habits
This species consumes small marine animals, crustaceans, mollusks, and insect larvae. They particularly favor marine worms, which minimizes competition with other shorebirds.

Migration Habits
Usually seen along the Pacific, Gulf, and Atlantic Coasts, these birds breed across northern Canada. If they migrate too early, finding the tundra marshes still frozen, they may head south for a few more weeks.

Placement of Feeders
In winter dunlins form large flocks of up to tens of thousands, but they do not mingle with other species. They are tame and can be approached quite easily.

brown

Fox Sparrow

D uring spring migration, the otherwise elusive fox sparrow conspicuously spouts loud, melodious warblings from a shrub or thicket. This sparrow—a separate genus from other sparrows—has 18 different subspecies in North America.

Description

Western birds are brownish or slate-colored and red-striped. Eastern birds are fox colored with orange-red wings and tail and blue-gray highlights on the head. The Rockies version is gray above with a reddish tail. All measure approximately 7.5 inches.

Preferred Habitat

As a ground nester, the sparrow makes its home in dense woodland thickets, overgrown coniferous forests, or in grassy pastures or roadsides.

Feeding Habits

Equipped with unusually large feet and claws, the fox sparrow, like the Eastern towhee, finds its meals by noisily double scratching among leaves for seeds, berries, or insects.

Migration Habits

Though most of its breeding range is found throughout the Rocky Mountain range, this sparrow winters in the Deep South and all along the West Coast.

Placement of Feeders

A smacking *tssk!* call or noisy scratching in leaves reveals the backyard presence of this shy visitor. Red cedars or elderberry bushes draw the sparrows in winter.

RANGE MAP

LEGEND

Summer Year-round
Winter Migration

Named for its insect-like song, a male grasshopper sparrow perches on a dried weed stalk singing *kip-kip-kip-zeee*, then flits off to chase a female, emitting sounds too high-pitched for human hearing. The clever female can make a display of injury to lure away predators, and conceals the location of the nest by walking to it through tall grass.

Description

This small grassland sparrow, measuring only 5 inches, is dark, scaly-patterned rust above, with a buff breast, pale stripe on crown, short pointed tail, and dark eyes.

Preferred Habitat

Grassland options vary by region, but the grasshopper sparrow prefers open, weedy meadows or pastures, including airports. These birds are sensitive to change, and their populations decline

brown

as overgrown fields are cleared for urban development.

Feeding Habits

Foraging among grass clumps, this bird eats seeds, spiders, grasshoppers, and other insects.

Migration Habits

The northern two-thirds of the United States (and, rarely, Florida) are breeding grounds for the bird, where they nest in loose colonies. When the weather turns, they winter across parts of the southern United States.

Placement of Feeders

If you have the option, mow or cultivate paddocks and hayfields late in summer to avoid destroying their ground-level nests.

RANGE MAP

LEGEND

- ■ Summer
- ■ Winter
- ■ Year-round
- ■ Migration

In a scraggly tree, on the barren Arctic tundra, a male gray-cheek pipes its sweet, fluting song for up to 20 hours of daylight. Unfortunately for North American birders, these birds are fairly quiet during migration and are heard less often than the Swainson's or Hermit thrushes.

Description

This 8-inch thrush is dull brown or olive-brown above and whitish below, with large dark spots on the breast and neck. The species is named for its gray cheek patch.

Preferred Habitat

In stark contrast to their South American, rainforest wintering grounds, the birds breed in sub-Arctic woodlands and willow and alder thickets. Females construct a nest of mud and plants near or on the ground.

Feeding Habits

The ground-foraging thrush ingests mainly ants, but also spiders, earthworms, caterpillars, mollusks, beetles, and fruit.

Migration Habits

This bird's bi-annual journey of up to 8,000 miles is a greater distance than any other thrush travels. Like the Swainson's thrush, this nighttime migrant risks collisions with tall buildings and TV towers.

Placement of Feeders

In spring and autumn, the gray-cheeked species is common and widespread, but easily overlooked as it spends most of its time quietly foraging on the ground.

RANGE MAP

LEGEND

■ Summer ■ Year-round
■ Winter ■ Migration

A lovely, hymn-like fluting song at twilight has earned the hermit thrush much admiration. Its long, rolling notes vary in pitch and volume, making it difficult to pinpoint the songster.

Description

The 7.5-inch thrush is olive-brown above and boldly spotted buff below. The face is gray with a white eye ring, but the best field mark is its reddish tail.

Preferred Habitat

This forest bird can be found in coniferous or deciduous woodlands or wooded swamps, bogs, and fields. The female builds a well-concealed ground nest, and the male helpfully feeds his incubating mate.

Feeding Habits

In spring and summer the bird forages on the ground and gleans vegetation for ants, butterflies, bees, moths, and spiders. In winter they subsist on wild fruits, buds, and berries.

Migration Habits

If you spot a spotted thrush in winter, it must be the hermit thrush. This species winters across the southern United States, but as soon as beetles emerge in early spring, they head north into the Rocky Mountain range and along the Pacific Coast.

Placement of Feeders

Suet cakes, raw apples, pecans, and peanut butter may attract this woodland bird to a backyard feeder. Watch for its characteristic tail-bobbing; this is the only thrush to wag its tail.

RANGE MAP

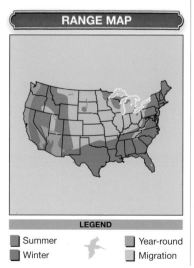

LEGEND

- Summer
- Winter
- Year-round
- Migration

brown

Horned Lark

brown

Of the world's 75 true lark species, the horned lark is the only one widespread in North America. The clearing of Eastern forests made way for this bird of open spaces, which often makes its home on prairies, air fields, farmland, or Arctic tundra.

Description
Although its black "horns" are rarely visible, the 8-inch lark is very distinct with its black markings on the head and black crescent band across the breast. The face is white or yellow and the black tail is rimmed with white.

Preferred Habitat
In a spectacular courtship display, males soar to heights of up to 800 feet, then nose-dive silently back down. Their nests—in a shallow depression on the bare ground—are vulnerable to late storms or spring planting.

Feeding Habits
Walking slowly along the ground and scratching with its large feet, the horned lark searches for grain, seeds, insects, or spiders.

Migration Habits
This bird breeds across most of the United States; its yearly migration takes it to the West Coast.

Placement of Feeders
Larks gather in flocks of up to thousands in late autumn, often joining with longspurs and buntings. They may be seen along roadsides or croplands, often singing in flight.

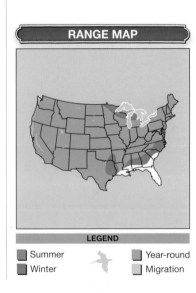

RANGE MAP

LEGEND
Summer   Year-round
Winter   Migration

In an effort to control crop pests, house sparrows were imported from England in 1850 and released all over the United States. They have since spread throughout the entire continent, where they thrive in human-altered environments (part of their Latin name is *domesticus*). Unfortunately, these aggressive competitors have diminished the success of native cavity nesters such as bluebirds and tree swallows.

Description

Males, up to 6.5 inches long, have a gray crown and rump, black bib, white cheeks, and chestnut head stripes, while the female and young are streaky brown above and white below.

Preferred Habitat

Resourceful and friendly, the house sparrow is at home in cities, suburbs, and farmland, where it constructs nests of grass, feathers, and bits of rubbish in a man-made or natural cavity.

Feeding Habits

The sparrow squabbles fiercely over territory, mates, and food, the latter including insects, grains, berries, and weed seeds.

Migration Habits

Some birds of the past experienced involuntary migration, touring the country by rail while snacking on spilled grain in train cars, but the house sparrow has become an abundant permanent resident throughout North America.

Placement of Feeders

A familiar sight at every backyard feeder, house sparrows are drawn to bread crumbs, seeds, and grain.

RANGE MAP

LEGEND

Summer

Winter

Year-round

Migration

brown

brown

Nearly every vacant lot or golf course is home to this noisy plover. When threatened, the adult bird feigns injury, dragging its wing as if broken, to lure predators away from the nest. These shorebirds flee by sprinting along the ground or swimming to safety.

Description
Named for its shrill *kill-deer* alarm call, the species measures 9–11 inches, colored brown above and white below, with a rust-colored rump, long legs, and a black-and-white tipped tail. Adults have two identifying black bands across the chest, though chicks have only one.

Preferred Habitat
Any short-grassed open field, river bank, or gravel road edge with water nearby can house the killdeer, where it nests in a shallow depression in the ground.

Feeding Habits
Like other plovers, killdeers feed with a stop-start action of chasing prey and standing still, then pecking in the dirt with their bills to seek seeds and insects, earthworms, and snails.

Migration Habits
As early as February, some killdeers migrate north to breed. However, they can be found from the East Coast to the West Coast throughout the year.

Placement of Feeders
Killdeers are common and easy to identify, but if you spot an adult male giving the broken-wing display, retreat and do not disturb them.

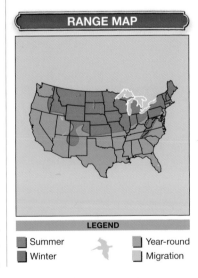

RANGE MAP

LEGEND

☐ Summer ☐ Year-round
☐ Winter ☐ Migration

The polygamous male builds up to 20 "dummy" nests to serve as courting sites for potential mates. Interested females then construct their own nests. This abundance of nests, most unused, makes it difficult for competing species to enact revenge when the marsh wren pierces the eggs of nearby wrens and larger blackbirds.

Description
Smaller than a sparrow at 4–5.5 inches, the wren is brown above, pale buff below, with a white-streaked back and white eyebrow. Males define and defend their territory with up to 200 different songs.

Preferred Habitat
The marsh wren prefers wetlands, particularly freshwater or brackish marshes with abundant cattails, bullrushes, or reeds. These plants are used

to construct a nest attached to reeds.

Feeding Habits
This flycatcher consumes aphids, beetles, wasps, bees, mites, and larval dragonflies, and plucks other aquatic insects and snails from their marshy home.

Migration Habits
This bird has an extensive breeding range spanning the United States from north to south. It can be found year-round, however, only along the Atlantic and Gulf Coasts and in the far West.

Placement of Feeders
Patient observation in the bird's habitat may be rewarded with a brief glimpse of its cocked tail. Listen for the male's call, reminiscent of a mechanical sewing machine.

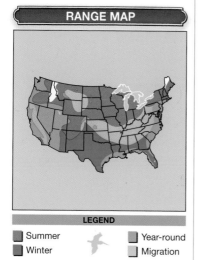

RANGE MAP

LEGEND

Summer

Winter

Year-round

Migration

brown

With 70 million shot annually, the mourning dove ranks as America's most popular game bird. The species boomed with the large-scale felling of forests, and its mournful *coo-ah, coo, coo* song is recognizable in all urban and suburban environments.

Description
This 12-inch sandy-colored dove has black wing spots and a long tapered tail bordered with white. Males are slightly brighter, with a pink sheen along the neck.

Preferred Habitat
The resilient mourning dove thrives from farmland to irrigated deserts, open fields, parks, and lawns. Their stick nests, built in tall trees, low bushes, or on the ground, are flimsy and poorly constructed, but home to at least two broods annually.

Feeding Habits
Like other doves and pigeons, this dove feeds its young regurgitated, protein-rich food known as "pigeon milk" produced in the adult's gullet. Birds may fly several miles at dawn or dusk in search of seeds, insects, or the nearest water source.

Migration Habits
Hundreds of birds may congregate for autumn migration from the southwest regions of Canada south throughout the continental United States.

Placement of Feeders
The backyard birder has only to listen for the dove's song to recognize this frequent feeder visitor. Watch for their fast silhouettes flying at early morning or dusk.

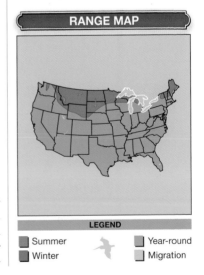

RANGE MAP

LEGEND

Summer Year-round

Winter Migration

A loud, repeated *flicker* or *wick-wick-wick* ringing in the forest canopy announces the breeding season of this unusual woodpecker. Three color variations exist—yellow-shafted (East), red-shafted (West), and gilded (Southwest)—but they interbreed where their ranges overlap.

Description

Large at 10-14 inches, flickers are black or brown with tan bars above, with a pale spotted breast and bright underwings. Eastern birds have yellow under the wings, a red nape, and a black "mustache" on males. Southwestern varieties have yellow underwings and a red mustache.

Preferred Habitat

Spot the flicker in open country near large trees, such as farmlands, parks,

brown

woodlands, deserts, and suburbs. They nest in a tree cavity or burrow into fence posts, rafters, or even saguaro cacti.

Feeding Habits

Foraging on the ground, the flicker extends its enormous tongue to lap up ants. It also consumes insects, fruit, and seeds, occasionally flycatching.

Migration Habits

Although year-round residents of the United States, these birds migrate north for the breeding season and return south to winter in south Texas and in the Desert Southwest.

Placement of Feeders

Watch for these ground feeders eating ants and beetles on lawns or sidewalks. They may also visit suet feeders.

RANGE MAP

LEGEND

- ◼ Summer
- ◼ Winter
- ◼ Year-round
- ◼ Migration

Feeding Habits

Harvesting seeds of hemlocks, alders, birches, and cedars is the siskin's primary objective, but insects make up a small part of its diet as well.

Migration Habits

Bird enthusiasts can look forward to the winter months, when the siskin spends its time the southeastern United States.

Placement of Feeders

Pine siskins, like other northern finches, are fond of salt and may be found along salted highways in winter. Thistle seeds are their feeder favorite, but backyard elm and ash trees can do the trick as well.

In the chilly autumn air, a flock of small, dark-colored birds undulates through the sky, alternately bunching up and fanning out. The distinctive, rising *bzzzzt* song confirms the presence of pine siskins.

Description

This 5-inch finch has a dark, streaked back, a notched tail, and small patches of yellow on the wings and tail. In flight it looks like a sparrow, but the splashes of yellow are good field markers.

Preferred Habitat

Small groups of pine siskins build their nests in conifers just a few feet apart. Here they raise two broods, then travel to mixed woodlands, alder thickets, or overgrown pastures in search of winter food.

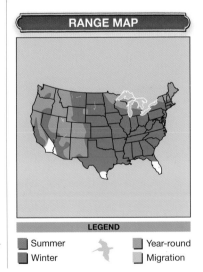

RANGE MAP

LEGEND

Summer   Year-round
Winter   Migration

From spring breeding season through autumn, and even into winter in the North, the aptly named song sparrow serenades his mate with more than 20 different songs, improvising more than 1,000 variations on these melodies.

Description

Coloring varies from rust to gray to streaked brown above, but all measure 5–7 inches long, with a brown eyebrow and a central spot in a streaked white breast. Juveniles lack the central breast spot and may be mistaken for the savannah sparrow.

Preferred Habitat

Song sparrows make their homes in thickets, gardens, parks, and roadsides, where they raise up to three broods each year. Fledglings begin to develop

brown

their own song repertoire before they even leave the nest.

Feeding Habits

These ground feeders use their feet to rustle up insects, seeds, grain, and berries. In flight, watch the sparrow's characteristic pumping of its long, rounded tail.

Migration Habits

Traveling solo or in pairs, song sparrows are found throughout the United States year-round, but winter from the Deep South into the Desert Southwest.

Placement of Feeders

Although common and widespread in North America, a song sparrow at a backyard feeder is a rare occasion. But if you locate a nearby nesting pair, watch for them to return year after year.

RANGE MAP

LEGEND

- Summer
- Winter
- Year-round
- Migration

P raised by American author Henry David Thoreau as the most beautiful song of any bird, the male wood thrush sings his sweet, liquid melody *ee-o-lay, ee-o-lay* at dawn and again at dusk, sometimes joined by the female's equally lovely song from the nest.

Description

At up to 8.5 inches, the starling-sized wood thrush is the largest bird of its family in the East. Adults are olive-brown above and dark-spotted white below. The bird's face is streaked black and white, and its crown is reddish.

Preferred Habitat

In damp mature forests, parks, and gardens with large shade trees, the mating pair combines mud, grasses, and moss to craft a sturdy nest for the season's two broods. Nests are frequently parasitized by brown-headed cowbirds.

Feeding Habits

The thrush's springtime diet consists almost entirely of insects, such as beetles, ants, and butterflies, but by late summer it eats mainly plants, berries, and seeds.

Migration Habits

In late April flocks migrate from Central America to the Great Plains and east to the Atlantic.

Placement of Feeders

This is the only thrush to regularly nest near human dwellings, but they seldom visit feeding stations. They are welcome residents in gardens because they eat cutworms and beetles.

RANGE MAP

LEGEND

Summer   Year-round
Winter   Migration

This finch is commonly known as the wild canary for its appearance and song. As it hops along summer fields gleaning thistle seeds, the male bird's bright yellow and black plumage is unmistakable.

Description

The summer breeding male is easily recognized, with its lemon-yellow coloring, and black cap, wings, and tail. At 5 inches long, the female and winter male are significantly duller yellow with black wings and tail.

Preferred Habitat

Fields, groves, thickets, farmland, and weedy grasslands provide a steady supply of small insects and seeds year-round.

Feeding Habits

In spring, when insects are plentiful,

they account for up to 50% of the goldfinch's diet. Seeds are its main staple through late summer and autumn, with berries supplementing in winter.

Migration Habits

Spring is ideal breeding time in western states, but in the East, goldfinches commonly wait until late summer, when weed seeds are readily available. They travel in flocks of up to 20, but are hardy enough to winter across much of their normal range.

Placement of Feeders

Feeders offering nigel thistle seeds and sunflower seeds are sure to draw these birds to your yard, and they are frequent visitors during the winter months. The goldfinch also loves birdbaths.

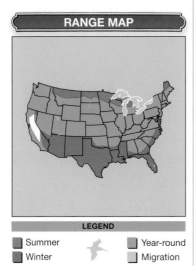

RANGE MAP

LEGEND

- Summer
- Winter
- Year-round
- Migration

yellow

mountain ranges, provide high perches for these foragers.

Feeding Habits
Like several other warblers, the Blackburnian warbler dines on insects and berries.

Migration Habits
Your best chance of spotting these otherwise elusive birds is from the last week of April through mid-May, as they migrate toward Canada and the Northeast in large flocks.

Placement of Feeders
These shy critters are best identified by their call and then sought among the high treetops, where they may appear at the ends of branches searching for bugs among the foliage.

Scientists recently discovered that although this warbler is similar to four other warblers that may share a common food source and even perch in the same conifer, each species uses different foraging techniques and lives at a different level from the ground.

Description
The spring male is streaked with black and white, with a bright orange throat, eyebrow, and crown patch. The female is similar but more yellow and grayish, with two identifying brace marks on her back. The 5-inch creature issues thin, fast, high-pitched calls *sleet-sleet-sleet* and *tiddly-tiddly-tiddly*.

Preferred Habitat
Coniferous forests, as well as oak-hickory woodlands in southeastern

RANGE MAP

LEGEND

Summer Year-round
Winter Migration

yellow

Until 1997, this bird was classified as a solitary vireo, but is now distinguished as a distinct species. The attractively colored blue-headed vireo is a fairly common migrant, seen earlier in the spring than other vireos. It is extremely tame and not threatened by human presence.

Description
Olive green above and white below with yellowish flanks, the 6-inch vireo features a slate blue head with bold white spectacle markings.

Preferred Habitat
The blue-headed species is the only vireo to inhabit coniferous forests, where it nests in the forked twigs of small trees.

Feeding Habits
Like other vireos (and distinct from

wrens), these slow fliers scan the trees for insects, hovering to pluck caterpillars, wasps, moths, butterflies, stink bugs, beetles, ants, spiders, or bees. Berries of dogwood trees may also catch this deliberate feeder's interest.

Migration Habits
Unique among vireos for their solo migrations, these birds are found in the eastern half of the United States, wintering in South Carolina and southward along the Gulf Coast.

Placement of Feeders
Friendly and fearless, these curious birds are comfortable on human territory. Listen for their slow, slurred calls. They have even been known to sit quietly and allow their feathers to be stroked.

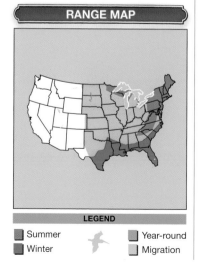

RANGE MAP

LEGEND

■ Summer		■ Year-round
■ Winter		■ Migration

yellow

Feeding Habits
Hovering low over a clump of cattails, the yellowthroat scoops up adult and larval insects such as spiders or dragonflies, supplementing its diet with seeds.

Migration Habits
Migrating from South and Central America into the entire United States during summer, this species is the northernmost yellowthroat in the western hemisphere. Though not its usual habitat, the migrating birds may be found far from water.

Placement of Feeders
This shy but curious species can be roused from their tall-grass hideouts by various noises. Try making a squeaking noise by kissing the back of your thumb, give a low growl, or make a *psssh-psssh* sound.

Often called the Maryland yellowthroat, where it was first collected in 1766, this sweet songbird is elusive and rarely seen. The male yellowthroat twitters from perch to perch, marking his territory and defending it aggressively.

Description
The small black-masked male issues a sharp *chek* call from his bright yellow throat. The 6-inch female, lacking the mask, responds with a gentle *wichity, wichity* song.

Preferred Habitat
Brushy swamps, wet thickets, or overgrown marshes, and tangles of weeds or berry bushes provide sufficient cover for the ground nests of these polygamous birds.

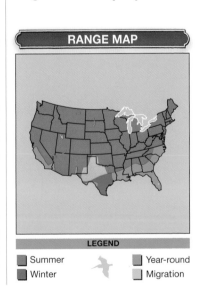

RANGE MAP

LEGEND

Summer

Winter

Year-round

Migration

Although actually in the blackbird family, the meadowlark is so named for its singing ability. The eastern and western meadowlarks are identical in appearance, habitat, and feeding and nesting habits, but have vastly different songs. A clear, high-pitched, wistful trill of *see seer seee-u* sets the eastern meadowlark apart from its western counterpart's longer, confident, gurgling song.

Description
Streaked black and brown on top and measuring 8–10.5 inches, this species has an eye-catching lemon yellow and black breast. The western species is paler and grayer.

Preferred Habitat
Weaving blades of prairie grass to make a dome, the female meadowlark constructs her ground nests in grasslands, pastures, and marshes. If the nest is destroyed by mowing, these polygamous breeders will nest again.

Feeding Habits
Grain and seeds round out a diet comprised mostly of insects, including spiders, beetles, grasshoppers, crickets, caterpillars, weevils, ants, and wasps.

Migration Habits
Traveling in groups, bright meadowlarks can be found in almost any grassy, open area. They occupy the eastern United States year-round, migrating slightly northward in summer.

Placement of Feeders
Look for these shy feeders perched on fence posts. They may be drawn to seeds and grain spread on the ground.

RANGE MAP

LEGEND

Summer
Winter
Year-round
Migration

yellow

species resides in overgrown fields and briar-rich pastures, abandoning fields when they become heavily forested.

Feeding Habits

The acrobatic warbler swings upside down to pick caterpillars and insects from the underside of foliage or hovers to snatch insects from leaves.

Migration Habits

Arriving in May, the warbler's short breeding season begins. By July, the fledglings leave the nest and the flocks return to South and Central America for the winter.

Placement of Feeders

If caterpillars are plentiful in your area, watch this colorful warbler consume mass quantities during April or September migration.

This bird is closely related to the blue-winged warbler, and these species interbreed where their ranges overlap, producing fertile hybrid offspring called Brewster's warblers; these offspring, in turn, produce Lawrence's warblers. The hybrid birds have coloring similar to either parent species, but with yellower bellies.

Description

Resembling a chickadee, the 4.5 inch male is gray above, white below, with a black mask and throat, yellow crown and wing patch, and white spots underneath the tail. The female has a gray mask and throat. From its perch within a briar patch, the warbler's insect-like song is a slow buzz.

Preferred Habitat

Generally preferring drier areas than the blue-winged warbler, this ground-nesting

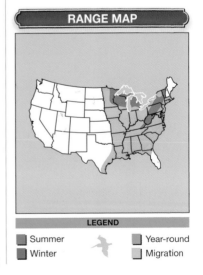

RANGE MAP

LEGEND

Summer Year-round
Winter Migration

yellow

The loud, clear whistling song of this colorful warbler makes them a welcome guest during spring and autumn migrations. Among wood warblers and within their own species, each bird has a specified habitat and feeding area or strategy, allowing peaceful coexistence with minimal competition.

Description

The handsome male, 5.5 inches long, is olive above and yellow below, with a yellow face and black hood and throat, while the duller female lacks the hood. Both have white tail spots that flash as they bound from branch to branch.

Preferred Habitat

In mature, mixed forests, especially ravines or wooded swamps, the warbler makes its home no more than 10 feet above the ground. Females produce two broods annually, as their low-lying nests are often predated by snakes.

Feeding Habits

Males catch flying insects and glean insect larvae from leaves and shrubs, while females hunt insects and spiders close to the ground.

Migration Habits

During their winters in the tropics, males and females select separate habitats, and only males return to the same mating grounds each year.

Placement of Feeders

Although not a likely visitor to suburban gardens, the hooded warbler is easiest to see during spring migration, in early to mid-April.

RANGE MAP

LEGEND

■ Summer
■ Winter
■ Year-round
■ Migration

yellow

yellow

Feeding Habits

This species has more diverse foraging methods than its relatives, alternately hopping along the ground, plucking caterpillars and spiders from foliage in the forest canopy, or chasing insects in flight.

Migration Habits

The bird was discovered in 1811 in Kentucky, but is no more common in that state than in the rest of its range. It summers in the East, migrating to the Yucatan Peninsula in September for winter.

Placement of Feeders

Listen for the male's rich, persistent *tur-dle, tur-dle* song during spring courtship. Unmated males often continue to sing throughout the summer.

T his shy bird spends the majority of its time foraging and skulking within dense shrubs or thickets, making it tough for all but the most persistent birder to spot.

Description

Olive above and bright yellow below, the 6-inch bird is best identified by its yellow spectacle markings and black forehead, crown, and cheek. Females have a gray crown and paler cheeks.

Preferred Habitat

Deciduous forest with ferns, briars, or other dense undergrowth is the ideal home for this warbler. The female incubates alone in a grassy nest on or near the ground, but the male abandons his soliloquies to help feed the chicks when they hatch.

RANGE MAP

LEGEND

■ Summer   ■ Year-round
■ Winter   ■ Migration

In an overgrown field, a startled brown sparrow flaps jerkily just above the grass, then dives back to the ground to flee on foot. This elusive sparrow, named for nineteenth-century naturalist John Le Conte, only risks emerging to a perch to share its insect-like song.

Description

Overall yellow-brown coloring makes this sparrow easy to identify. Adults measure 5 inches, with a white crown stripe, wide streaked red collar, gray patch above the ear, and a pointed tail. Nonbreeding birds are yellowish and duller.

Preferred Habitat

For breeding, Le Conte's sparrow favors grassland and meadows bordering marshland, especially fields containing foxtail, where it nests in a grass clump

on the ground. Dry, brushy fields are its home in winter.

Feeding Habits

A weak flyer, the bird scans the ground and low vegetation for seeds and insects, including grasshoppers, leafhoppers, and spiders.

Migration Habits

In the last century this sparrow's breeding range has shifted north, but it winters in the southeastern states.

Placement of Feeders

These stout sparrows are most numerous during their fall migration, though they rarely sing in this season. Unlike other sparrows, they can be approached quite closely when perched.

yellow

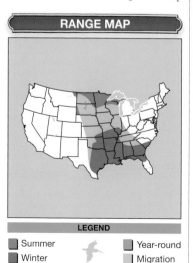

RANGE MAP

LEGEND

■ Summer
■ Winter
■ Year-round
■ Migration

Nashville Warbler

yellow

I n 1811, when Alexander Wilson discovered this warbler in Tennessee, the bird was not a common resident. But the clearing of vast forests generated the overgrown pasture favored by the Nashville warbler, now a common migrant throughout much of North America.

Description

This 5-inch warbler is olive above and bright yellow below, with a white patch on the belly between the legs. The male's pearly gray head has a white eye ring and a usually concealed red crown patch. Females have an olive-colored head and a blue-gray neck.

Preferred Habitat

During migration the warbler can be found in woodlands, shrubs, and suburbs, while it breeds in brushy fields, young woodlands, and groves. Its ground nest is securely hidden under a sapling or shrub, or in a clump of moss.

Feeding Habits

This insectivore scours leaves and flowering plants for spiders, beetles, aphids, caterpillars, flies, and grasshoppers.

Migration Habits

Highly localized populations breed throughout California north to Washington and from Minnesota across New England. Most winter in Mexico, but small groups remain along the coasts of California and Texas.

Placement of Feeders

Watch for this iridescent warbler during spring migration. Its two-part song is a high-pitched *see-it, see-it, see-it* followed by *ti-ti-ti-ti*.

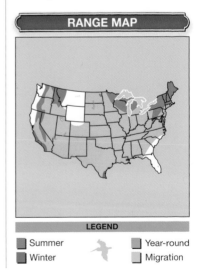

RANGE MAP

LEGEND

Summer   Year-round
Winter   Migration

Like the American tree sparrow, this bird is not found in the habitat its name would suggest. This small songbird prefers second-growth forests that spring up following logging or burning.

Description

Tiny at 4 inches, the warbler is olive-green above and yellow below, with two white bars on dark wings and a dark eye stripe. Males have rusty stripes down the back, and females have olive rather than black stripes on the face.

Preferred Habitat

This warbler prefers young stands of pine, deciduous saplings, or mangroves. The nest is a cup of plant down in a low tree or shrub. Like some other warblers, females commonly eat the eggshells (a source of calcium) after their young hatch.

Feeding Habits

This insectivore occasionally catches flying insects on the wing, but generally gleans grasshoppers and spiders from foliage.

Migration Habits

In early spring the prairie warbler leaves its home in the Caribbean and heads north to breed in the East and South, from Texas to Maine.

Placement of Feeders

No other olive-backed yellow warbler shares this bird's habit of "wagging" its tail while perched. Listen for both versions of the male's rapid, buzzy song, one to court females and the other to warn away competitors.

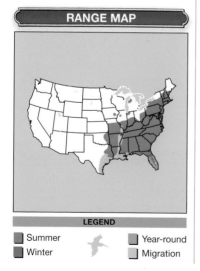

RANGE MAP

LEGEND

- Summer
- Winter
- Year-round
- Migration

yellow

Worm-eating Warbler

T his bird spends most of its time quietly scouring the leaf litter and low vegetation for insects and moth larvae. Males sing their rapid, insect-like buzz from a high perch but sit motionless for a long time, making them difficult to spot.

yellow

Description
Both males and females are plain brown above with black and yellow crown stripes, measuring 5.5 inches. If spotted, they freeze, relying on their coloring for camouflage.

Preferred Habitat
Dry, wooded ravines and steep forest hillsides are the best places to locate these woodland warblers. Their nests, constructed of dead leaves on the ground, are frequently cleaned of parasites by brown-headed cowbirds.

Feeding Habits
Spiders and slugs are the bird's main diet in spring, while caterpillars and other insects vary its menu in summer and autumn. Primarily the warbler forages on the ground, but also gleans insects from trees and shrubs.

Migration Habits
In summer breeding season, this elusive bird nests south to Texas and North Carolina, migrating for the tropics as the weather turns chill.

Placement of Feeders
Even legendary ornithologist John J. Audubon never found a worm-eating warbler's nest in his lifetime, but you can listen for their *zeep-zeep* call rising from the wooded hillsides during spring.

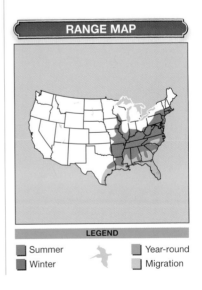

RANGE MAP

LEGEND

■ Summer   ■ Year-round
■ Winter   ■ Migration

A flash of bright yellow flitting into a backyard ornamental shrub may announce the presence of this 5-inch warbler, the only North American warbler to appear all yellow.

Description

Adult males are yellow-green above and bright yellow below, with two yellow tail patches and reddish stripes on the breast and belly. Juveniles and females are duller yellow to olive-green.

Preferred Habitat

A freshwater source and small trees are the ideal environment for yellow warbler colonies, commonly found in willow thickets, marshes, swamps, parks, and backyard gardens. Mating pairs construct strong nests in small trees. If parasitized by the brown-

headed cowbird, the warbler layers nest material over the unwelcome egg.

Feeding Habits

Like other warblers this species is entirely insectivorous. Males tend to search for food higher in the tree canopy than do the less conspicuous females.

Migration Habits

Traveling by night and resting by day, warbler flocks arrive in late April in the northern two-thirds of the United States. After a very short breeding season, the birds return to Mexico, and Central and South America for winter.

Placement of Feeders

The yellow warbler rarely visits feeding stations, but as flocks migrate south in late July, listen for their sweet, clear seven-note song.

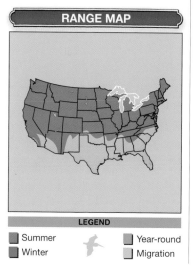

RANGE MAP

LEGEND

- Summer
- Winter
- Year-round
- Migration

yellow

yellow

This usually silent bird has a tendency to sing at the approach of a storm, earning it the nickname "rain crow." Its unique call is a rapid, rattling *ka-ka-ka-kow-kowp-kowp-kowp*.

Description

Slender and long-tailed, the bird measures 10–12.5 inches, colored brown above and white below with a yellow and black bill. In flight, note the large white spots under the tail and the red patches on the wings.

Preferred Habitat

The cuckoo crafts a flimsy twig nest in a bush or a small sapling in orchards, damp thickets, overgrown fields, or suburban parks. Although not classified as a nest parasite, the cuckoo will sometimes lay eggs in its black-billed relative's nest or those of other birds.

Feeding Habits

A taste for hairy caterpillars and tent worms makes this bird useful for keeping agricultural pests in check. Their varied diet also includes fruit and berries, small bird eggs, and tiny amphibians.

Migration Habits

In spring the cuckoos travel from their South American wintering grounds to parts of California, along the Rockies, north to Minnesota and east to the coast.

Placement of Feeders

Even backyard cuckoo residents are shy and easily overlooked, as they rarely draw attention to themselves. Watch for them in late summer during temporary swarms of cicadas.

RANGE MAP

LEGEND

■ Summer   ■ Year-round
■ Winter   ■ Migration

Formerly the yellow-rump was thought to be two species, the eastern myrtle warbler and the western Audubon's warbler. The breeding males of each region look distinct, but they interbreed freely.

Description
Breeding males, 5–6 inches long, are dull blue above streaked with black, with a black breast and flanks and bright yellow on the rump, crown, and sides. Eastern males have a white throat and two white wing bars, whereas western males have a yellow throat and a large white wing patch. Females and juveniles always have the yellow rump.

Preferred Habitat
For summer breeding these warblers prefer coniferous and mixed forests, forest edges, and overgrown and cultivated

fields, where they build bulky twig nests in conifers. During other seasons they forage in a variety of habitats.

Feeding Habits
Winter populations are heavily dependent on poison ivy berries, while summer birds consume insects and berries.

Migration Habits
The widespread warbler breeds from the Pacific Northwest to New England and south to Mexico in the western half of the country. Winter finds them roosting in pine forests from their breeding range to the tropics.

Placement of Feeders
In winter these birds frequent gardens but rarely visit feeders. Listen for their frequent *chip* call to distinguish them.

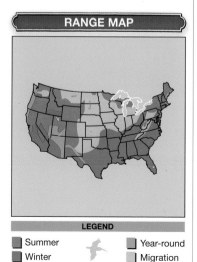

RANGE MAP

LEGEND

■ Summer ■ Year-round
■ Winter ■ Migration

yellow

blue

M ales of the species are easily identified, looking just as their name describes in both breeding and nonbreeding seasons. Unlike most warblers, the females look so unlike the males that early naturalists thought they were different species.

Description
Males are blue-gray above and on the crown, with a black face, bill, throat, and sides. Females are olive above and dark buff below with a small white patch on the wings. Both measure up to 5.5 inches long.

Preferred Habitat
Within a dense rhododendron or a mountain laurel, the mating pair constructs a nest near the ground with twigs, grass, ferns, and leaves. During migration, they are found in mixed forests with plenty of deciduous saplings.

Feeding Habits
Primarily an insectivore, the black-throated blue warbler gleans or fly-catches for caterpillars, spiders, moths, or other insects, but also consumes berries and seeds as available seasonally.

Migration Habits
This colorful warbler is found in the United States only in summer, from Wisconsin in a wide swath eastward to New England and south to Florida.

Placement of Feeders
If American yew or the bird's preferred nesting shrubs are planted on your property you'll be able to observe these tame birds at close range.

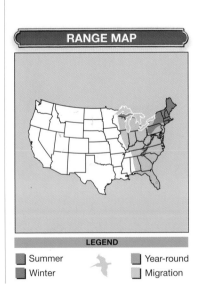

RANGE MAP

LEGEND

■ Summer   ■ Year-round
■ Winter   ■ Migration

These brightly colored, noisy birds have a mixed reputation. Both tame and curious, they warn other birds of danger and mob predators. Yet they also eat fledglings of other species and can imitate a hawk's screech or other bird calls to claim feeders for themselves.

Description
At 12.5 inches, this large bird has an unmistakable bright blue crest, back, wings, and tail, with white tail tips, face, and underparts. Issuing a repertoire of boisterous calls, its own soft *queedle-queedle* song is seldom heard.

Preferred Habitat
Jays inhabit forests of all kinds, but oak forests are preferred. They are also common residents of gardens and parks.

Feeding Habits
One of the few birds to cache food, the jay buries seeds and acorns for winter, indirectly planting new trees. Nuts, seeds, fruits, insects, mice, and bird fledglings comprise its diet.

Migration Habits
Traveling in flocks, these birds can be found from the eastern slopes of the Great Rocky Mountains to the Atlantic Coast. Its counterpart west of the Rockies is Steller's Jay.

Placement of Feeders
These backyard bullies are frequent feeder visitors in winter, and they love sunflower seeds, suet, cracked corn, and peanuts. They are comfortable around humans, but may mob birds, squirrels, cats, or even great horned owls.

blue

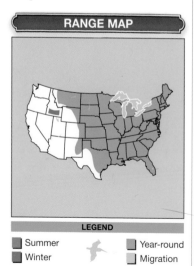

RANGE MAP

LEGEND

■ Summer ■ Year-round
■ Winter ■ Migration

The incessantly active gnatcatcher cocks and flicks its long tail as it bounds through the branches. These tiny birds are fearless, readily attacking crows, jays, or other large predators who threaten their territory.

Description

Measuring 4–5.5 inches, the gnatcatcher is blue-gray above and white below with a long, black tail edged with white. Breeding males have an identifying black eyebrow, but in winter their gray eyebrow matches the female's.

Preferred Habitat

In summer the bird is at home in open mixed woodlands, especially juniper groves. Its tiny lichen-decorated nest hooked to thin twigs is often parasitized by brown-headed cowbirds. As mating pairs take turns incubating the eggs or feeding the fledglings, the male warbles incessantly at top volume.

Feeding Habits

This quick flyer can pursue fleeing insects through the treetops, hover to pick insects and spiders from leaves or flowers, or snatch tiny gnats from the air. In autumn they join mixed foraging flocks.

Migration Habits

Breeding throughout most of the United States, gnatcatchers can be found in summer or year-round in The South.

Placement of Feeders

Track down this hyperactive bird by following its nasal *meehr* or buzzy *spee* call. Their high-pitched song will lead you right to their nest, which they don't attempt to conceal.

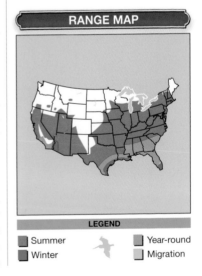

RANGE MAP

LEGEND

Summer
Winter
Year-round
Migration

blue

Although notoriously tough for bird-watchers to identify with any certainty because they live high in the forest canopy, try listening for series of quick, accelerating buzzing sounds and a higher buzzing drone to indicate the presence of these warblers. They may soon be added to the threatened species list as populations have reduced drastically in much of their range.

Description
Aptly named for its coloring, the 5-inch adult male is light blue above and white below, with a dark breast band. The female and juvenile look similar but are often tinged with green, lacking streaks or the breast band.

Preferred Habitat
Rich deciduous and mixed forests are the habitat of choice for this warbler. Females construct nests on long branches of box elder trees, where their coloring provides good camouflage.

Feeding Habits
In the highest levels of the forest, these shy birds rummage in foliage for insects such as caterpillars.

Migration Habits
Unlike most birds, the cerulean warbler has a discontinuous range, breeding in loose colonies across the Northeast and Midwest and wintering in the tropics.

Placement of Feeders
The cerulean species is difficult to distinguish from other warblers, but with careful observation it can be sighted singing in treetops from dawn to dusk.

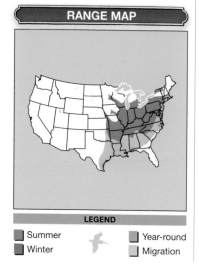

RANGE MAP

LEGEND
- Summer
- Winter
- Year-round
- Migration

blue

Feeding Habits

From a low perch, the bluebird swoops to snatch up insects, particularly spiders and grasshoppers, which comprise 80% of its diet. Berries provide extra sustenance in winter months.

Migration Habits

Inhabiting the southern half of its breeding range year-round, populations may be threatened by long freezes. They nest in woodpecker holes, birdhouses, or other safe cavities, where the young of the season's first brood help raise the second.

Placement of Feeders

Monitor your bluebird houses to prevent habitation by aggressive starlings. The easily tamed bluebirds love birdbaths and are drawn to feeders offering peanut butter or a shallow dish of mealworms.

I n forests east of the Rockies, a gentle bird whispers a sweet *tru-al-ly* song from its perch in a pine. Although once widespread, the eastern bluebird has been crowded out of nesting sites by starlings and house sparrows. Its regeneration depends largely on man-made bluebird houses.

Description

The male, 5–7 inches long, is bright blue above, with a rusty orange throat and white belly. The paler female has a brown-ringed back and rusty throat.

Preferred Habitat

In summer, look for them near pines, orchards, open woodlands, or on mountain slopes. Forming family groups in winter, they roost in grassland or farmland.

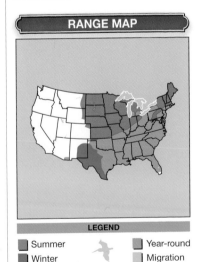

RANGE MAP

LEGEND

Summer — Year-round
Winter — Migration

D uring spring migration, from late March to early May, the colorful male finch, giving sharp *chip* calls in flight, is a common and welcome sight.

Description

Though similar to house finches and Cassin's finches, purple finches have a bluish-purple hue. Males, 5.5–6.5 inches long, are bluish-purple above and below, fading to a pale stomach. The sparrow-like female is brown, heavily streaked below, with whitish markings on her face.

Preferred Habitat

These finches usually nest in conifers, but that may include ornamental conifers in gardens or parks. They are also found in mixed and coniferous woodlands and bottomland forests.

RANGE MAP

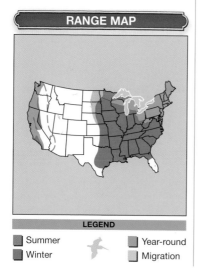

LEGEND

■ Summer	■ Year-round
■ Winter	■ Migration

Feeding Habits

Finches thrive on box elder, ash, and sycamore seeds, as well as maple, birch, and aspen buds. Fruit and berries provide sustenance in winter, and insects are a treat in summer.

Migration Habits

Generally these birds breed across most of Canada, but can also be found year-round along the Pacific Coast. But when food in the northern forests is scarce, purple finches flood their southern range.

Placement of Feeders

Year after year, small groups of purple finches return to their favorite feeders, especially those featuring sunflower seeds, where these birds lend a splash of color and a rich, cheery song to the winter landscape.

blue

American Redstart

A n Old English word for tail is "start" and the male's bright, reddish tail, which he constantly flashes and fans, earns the name. In their Latin American wintering grounds, redstarts are known as *candelita*, or "little flame."

Description

Adult males, at about 5 inches, are glossy black with flame-colored patches on the tail, wings, and sides year-round. Females and young males are pale olive to dark gray above with bright yellow highlights and a white belly.

Preferred Habitat

Redstarts make their home in mixed and deciduous second-growth forests along swamps or streams. The season's brood is raised in a tree-bound nest of moss and grass.

Feeding Habits

Restless and active, these small birds are always in motion, scanning foliage for tiny berries, dropping to the ground to munch on seeds, then zooming away to chase an insect with the aid of bristly feathers around the beak.

Migration Habits

Wintering south of the border, the breeding ground for the American Redstart consist of most the continental United States.

Placement of Feeders

Watch for a flash of black and orange in the treetops to find these common warblers, who usually respond with interest to birders making a "pishing" or squeaking sound.

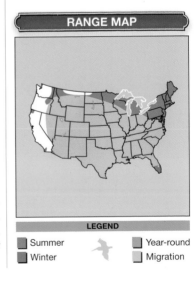

RANGE MAP

LEGEND

■ Summer ■ Year-round
■ Winter ■ Migration

black

This and the western Bullock's oriole are sometimes classified as the same species, the northern oriole. With the planting of trees across the Great Plains, their ranges overlapped and these distinct-looking birds began to interbreed.

Description

Males are unmistakable, with their black back and head, bright orange belly, black wings barred with white, and orange in the wings and tail. Females have a hint of orange. Juveniles look like females, and the juveniles of both races are nearly identical.

Preferred Habitat

In May the oriole constructs a pendulous pouch nest in the fork of a shade tree to raise its annual brood. In winter look for their beautifully woven nests in bare branches as evidence of their

summer residences.

Feeding Habits

Seated in the forest canopy the oriole collects caterpillars, insects, and mulberries, then swoops to ground level to drain nectar from flowers.

Migration Habits

These orioles breed in the East, with the Bullock's covering the West and into Canada. In early September, they migrate south to winter in Mexico and South America.

Placement of Feeders

Before you sight them you will likely hear their clear, whistled *tea-dear-dear-dear* song. The best backyard draws are orange halves, grape jelly, suet, and nectar feeders.

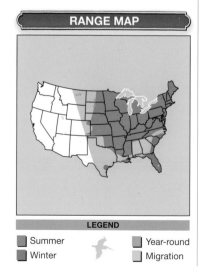

RANGE MAP

LEGEND

■ Summer
■ Winter
■ Year-round
■ Migration

black

Long ago abandoning natural nesting sites for docks, bridges, and barns, this swallow is a common sight in rural and suburban communities. Its forked tail is easily recognizable in flight, and it's the only swallow that flaps continuously, issuing a constant stream of twittering and chattering.

Description

Measuring 5-7 inches long, with a deeply forked tail and pointed wings, the barn swallow is dark blue-black above, with a red throat and pale undersides. Its flight is fast and direct, and may skim close to the ground.

Preferred Habitat

This bird favors open country or marshes near buildings and water, such as golf courses, parks, and farms. It constructs nest made of mud pellets under building eaves or on a beam.

Feeding Habits

They capture insects on the wing, and thus spend more time in flight than almost any other bird. Like other swallows, they skim the surface of rivers or lakes to drink while flying.

Migration Habits

Wintering outside the United States presents no great challenge, as the swallow travels up to 600 miles or more to reach its summer breeding grounds throughout the lower 48 states of the U.S.

Placement of Feeders

Encourage the presence of these helpful insectivores by allowing them to nest in buildings or other man-made structures.

RANGE MAP

LEGEND

Summer

Winter

Year-round

Migration

black

Destruction of its marsh habitat has led to drastically reduced populations of these elegant terns. Since its appearance on the Audubon Society's Blue List of threatened species in 1971, efforts continue to preserve and protect its wetland home.

Description

This large bird, measuring 9–10.5 inches, is unmistakable in all seasons. Breeding adults are all black, with a grayish tail and white highlights on the wings. Winter birds are gray above, with a black cap, and patchy white below with white side patches.

Preferred Habitat

Alongside freshwater marshes, lagoons, and lakes, black terns build a small hollow nest on floating marsh plants. Social and gregarious, these terns usually nest and roost in colonies numbering a few to hundreds of birds.

Feeding Habits

This tern occasionally dives into freshwater for fish and crustaceans, but spends most of its time swooping erratically after flying insects.

Migration Habits

Their summer breeding range stretches from California to New England and north throughout Canada. In autumn they head south and seaward, wintering at sea or along the coasts of Central America, South America, or even far-flung Africa.

Placement of Feeders

Watch for this carnivore feeding along inland lakes and marshes. Listen for their nasal song or short *kik* call.

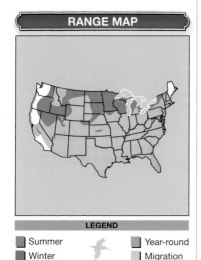

RANGE MAP

LEGEND

■ Summer
■ Winter
■ Year-round
■ Migration

black

at the base of a tree, shrub, rock, or log.

Feeding Habits
Even before the spring leaves unfold, this warbler scours branches and tree trunks upside down, poking into loose bark for insects and larvae, especially spiders and daddy longlegs.

Migration Habits
As early as March, flocks appear in the East, heading north to breed throughout Canada. By July the birds are ready to head south, wintering along parts of the Gulf Coast to South America.

A thin, 5-inch bird striped black and white all over creeps down a tree trunk. Sometimes nicknamed the black-and-white creeper or nuthatch for its unusual tree-creeping habits, this unmistakable zebra-patterned bird is the oddball of the warbler family.

Placement of Feeders
Track down their high-pitched, creaky-hinge song of six to eight *wee-see* phrases to observe this cooperative, friendly warbler.

Description
The male has a black mask and throat in summer, but in winter the throat is white. Females have a white face and throat with a black stripe through the eye. Juveniles are patterned with brown instead of black.

Preferred Habitat
In deciduous and mixed forests of the North and East, these warblers can be found building grass nests concealed with dead leaves on or near the ground

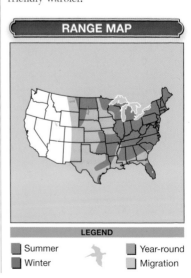

RANGE MAP

LEGEND

Summer   Year-round

Winter   Migration

black

As its name suggests, this heron is most active at night, but can often be seen during daylight feeding along edges of lakes and lagoons or roosting in trees. At sundown, when most herons return to the nest, these birds leave their roosts and set out to hunt.

Description

Hunched and stocky, the night heron measures 22–28 inches. Adults have a black cap and back, red eyes, gray wings, yellow legs, and a white belly. Streaky gray juveniles closely resemble the American bittern.

Preferred Habitat

In marshes, rivers, or wooded swamps, this heron piles up a mass of sticks to craft a messy platform nest. These fragile constructions are often disrupted by

storms or high winds, dumping the chicks unceremoniously on the rubble below the rookery.

Feeding Habits

Silent and menacing, the heron perches on the edge of a pond or marsh waiting for its aquatic prey—frogs, fish, and crustaceans—to chance within range.

Migration Habits

This heron summers throughout almost all states and north into central Canada, and remains year-round along the Pacific, Gulf, and Atlantic Coasts.

Placement of Feeders

Its scientific name, *nycticorax*, means "night raven." Listen for this bird's loud, barking *squawk*, a common nighttime sound.

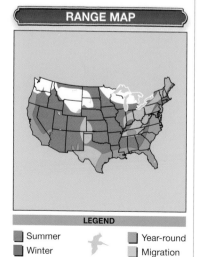

RANGE MAP

LEGEND

- Summer
- Winter
- Year-round
- Migration

black

feathers to keep the fledglings warm.

Feeding Habits

Gleaning from foliage or flycatching, the blackpoll consumes caterpillars, spiders, wasps, aphids, mosquitoes, and other insects. In their wintering grounds, the warblers subsist on nectar, fruit, and pollen.

Migration Habits

Crossing thousands of miles each spring and autumn, the blackpoll warbler faces many dangers. They rest and feed by day and migrate at night, often crashing head-on into tall buildings, TV towers, and lighthouses.

Weighing only half an ounce, the 6-inch blackpoll warbler is America's only small land bird to make the transoceanic journey of 10,000 miles between northern Canada and the rainforests of northeast South America, crossing vast stretches of the Atlantic Ocean and Gulf of Mexico.

Placement of Feeders

The blackpolls are very late migrants through the United States, commonly resting and feeding in oak forests.

Description

Breeding males are streaked black and white, with a black crown and throat and white cheeks. Females, juveniles, and nonbreeding males are greenish with pale legs.

Preferred Habitat

In the spruce forests of Canada's Far North, these hardy birds craft a secure cup of twigs, stems, and grass in a spruce or fir tree, lining the nest with

black

Named by John J. Audubon for the nineteenth-century ornithologist Thomas M. Brewer, this blackbird happily makes its home among humans in urban developments. As it trots along the ground, its head jerks back and forth like a chicken's.

Description

The male is solid black, up to 10 inches long, with a glossy purple-blue head. The female is dull gray with dark eyes. An excited blackbird makes an array of gurgles, squawks, and whistles, while its creaking song is *k-shee*.

Preferred Habitat

Open country, farmyards, parks, and lawns provide ample food and ideal nesting conditions. Colonies of up to 30 pairs may nest in hay fields, where

the young are fledged before harvest time, or in conifers.

Feeding Habits

A year-round diet of insects and seeds is supplemented in autumn when Brewer's blackbirds swarm granaries and farms to feast on spilled grain.

Migration Habits

In summer these birds breed in small colonies, but when the fledglings can fly, they join up with neighboring colonies and flocks of red-wings, cowbirds, starlings, and grackles to form a migratory mob of tens of thousands of birds.

Placement of Feeders

Scatter seed or grain on the ground for these blackbirds to peck at.

RANGE MAP

LEGEND

- Summer
- Winter
- Year-round
- Migration

black

Feeding Habits
Scanning the ground, scouring trees or shrubs, or wading in water, this blackbird seeks insects, seeds, fruit, grain, salamanders, eggs, or fish, and will consume the young of other birds, reducing its popularity with bird lovers.

Migration Habits
Found year-round in the South and Midwest, these late migrants congregate by the thousands in late autumn and early spring. Attempts to control their huge flocks have been unsuccessful.

Placement of Feeders
Backyard feeders and public garbage bins alike are subject to raids by these aggressive scavengers. Cracked corn, mixed seeds, suet, and sunflower hearts are sure-fire lures.

Ironically classified as a songbird because it shares with those species a special resonating voice box, the grackle is known for its piercing, high-pitched screech. Its harsh call is reflected in its name, derived from the Latin *graculous* meaning "to cough."

Description
A large bird measuring up to 12.5 inches, the grackle has a long, wedge-shaped tail and yellow eyes. Males appear iridescent bronze or black with purple, greenish, or bronze highlights, while the female is less glossy and shorter tailed.

Preferred Habitat
Grackles are common in groves, towns, farmland, marshes, thickets, or suburban landscapes, where food is plentiful.

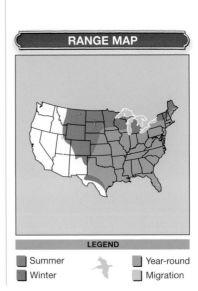

RANGE MAP

LEGEND
Summer
Winter
Year-round
Migration

D ownies are the smallest and friendliest of the North American woodpeckers. Like their tree-hammering relatives, a strong bill, neck, and reinforced skull protect the brain from repeated hammering, and bristly feathers protect the nostrils.

Description

This species is a 7-inch version of the hairy woodpecker. The back and belly are white, the black wings spotted white, and the tail barred. Males have a red patch on the head, and both have a thin black mustache.

Preferred Habitat

Any urban or rural area with deciduous trees can be home to this small woodpecker. Mating pairs excavate a cavity in a tree, stump, or fence post to build the nest. Parents share incubation

and feeding duties.

Feeding Habits

Foraging among foliage and under bark with its sharply barbed tongue, the bird consumes insects, larvae, and grubs. In winter they can be found in weedy fields, consuming dormant wasps and corn-borers.

Migration Habits

The downy is found in almost all of North America, remaining in the North all winter to forage among frozen fields and backyards.

Placement of Feeders

Feeding stations featuring berries, beef suet, peanut butter, pecans, or sunflower seeds will be home to plucky downies, especially in winter.

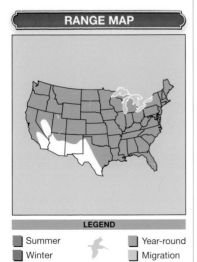

RANGE MAP

LEGEND

- Summer
- Winter
- Year-round
- Migration

black

Feeding Habits

For most of the year its diet consists entirely of flying insects, but in winter it subsists on the fruit and berries of poison ivy and poison sumac, and may even scoop little fish from shallow water.

Migration Habits

This hardy flycatcher has a long breeding season in the East and central Canada, with most wintering in the Southeast and in Mexico.

Placement of Feeders

Although tame and common in suburbs and farmland, the eastern phoebe rarely visits feeding stations. The best field mark is the constant downward "wagging" of its long tail.

From its perch on a dead branch, an unremarkable 7-inch bird sweetly chants *fee-bee* over and over. Suddenly a flying insect catches its eye, and it darts out to snatch it, returning swiftly to its favorite perch.

Description

This phoebe is best distinguished from other flycatchers by its lack of wing bars or eye ring. It is gray-brown or olive above and white below, with a black bill.

Preferred Habitat

Phoebes prefer to live near a freshwater source but are well adapted to living among human developments. They attach mud nests to vertical walls, barn rafters, windowsills, and bridge supports. Hard-working females raise two broods each season.

RANGE MAP

LEGEND

Summer Year-round
Winter Migration

black

Birders have no trouble recognizing a small "teapot" of towhees with their short, bounding flight and distinct *drink your tea* call. Formerly this species was grouped with the spotted towhee under the name rufous-sided towhee.

Description

This large, boldly colored sparrow measures 7–9 inches, with white marks on the wings and tail that look like streamers in flight. The male is black above, with a black chest, a white belly, and red flanks, while the female is brown above.

Preferred Habitat

Abandoned fields, brushy forest edges, and oak or palmetto forests with dense undergrowth are safe environments for the shy towhee, where it nests on the ground. If the season's first brood

is destroyed, a second nest will be constructed in a bush or tree.

Feeding Habits

Hopping, digging, and kicking with both feet, the towhee rustles up insects, spiders, seeds, and berries among leaf litter and soil, earning its nickname "ground robin."

Migration Habits

This solitary bird travels alone or in pairs between its wintering range and summer breeding grounds slightly northward.

Placement of Feeders

In spring and summer, watch for towhee pairs double scratching for dropped seeds under your ground feeders.

RANGE MAP

LEGEND

- ■ Summer
- ■ Winter
- ■ Year-round
- ■ Migration

black

In 1890 a Shakespeare enthusiast released 100 starlings in New York City in an effort to introduce all feathered friends mentioned in Shakespeare's works. Now numbering 200 million, starlings are noisy and messy, but they consume a large quantity of insects.

Description

Shiny black with a green or purple sheen in summer, the bird molts in autumn, growing a winter coat of white-speckled feathers. The stout, 7.5-inch starling is a skillful imitator known for its wolf-whistle call.

Preferred Habitat

Especially common around landfills or grain elevators, the starling is at home in cities, suburbs, or farmland. The female constructs a nest of twigs and trash in a tree or cavity.

Feeding Habits

City dwellers and rural residents alike can spot these birds probing for insects, spiders, worms, fruit, grain, or seeds from parks to farmyards.

Migration Habits

This native of Eurasia is found year-round from central Canada to northern Mexico. During colder months, they fly in enormous swarms to roost in warmer downtown areas.

Placement of Feeders

Starlings are drawn to seed and suet feeders, but if you intend your nest boxes for native species such as bluebirds, woodpeckers, or purple martins, monitor them carefully for starling habitation.

RANGE MAP

LEGEND

Summer

Winter

Year-round

Migration

The first flycatcher ever classified by American ornithologists was found in Acadia, an old name for Nova Scotia. Later, several of these similar-looking species were distinguished and renamed. This bird retains the original moniker, despite the fact that its northernmost range lies in Connecticut.

Description

Adults measure 6.5 inches long, with olive green plumage above, a white throat and yellow belly, two pale wing bars, and a bold yellow eye ring. The greenish juvenile has a scaly appearance.

Preferred Habitat

Mature, deciduous forests or bottomland swamps are the best locales to seek the Acadian. In a maple or beech tree, the female builds a loose nest high above the ground, often

over water or paved roads.

Feeding Habits

This insectivore hovers above branches or leaves seeking spiders, bees, wasps, ants, and insect larvae. Small fruits and berries supplement their diet in winter.

Migration Habits

In North America the Acadian flycatcher is a summer visitor, appearing in late April for breeding from eastern Texas northward and east to the coast.

Placement of Feeders

These common migrants are active and aggressive, giving a stunning aerial courtship chase with a sharp *ti-ti-ti-ti* call. Also listen for their unique *peet-sa* call.

RANGE MAP

LEGEND

■ Summer   ■ Year-round
■ Winter   ■ Migration

gray

season. During nonbreeding season they can be found on dunes, plowed fields, and shores.

Feeding Habits
Walking slowly on sturdy legs, the pipit consumes insects, spiders, snails, mayflies, and dragonflies and their larvae. In winter it eats mainly seeds.

Migration Habits
In March males head to their breeding range in the Rocky Mountains north to Alaska and the Arctic Circle, while females follow in May. In September, flocks head south to the southern United States and Central and South America.

Tiny but hardy, the pipit nests only in the harsh tundra environment. American birders are likely to see them during migration, where they rest in mud flats and wet grain fields, though nesting pairs do appear throughout the Rocky Mountain range.

Placement of Feeders
The pipit seldom stops to perch, but listen for its quick *pipit* call in flight and observe its constant tail-bobbing action.

Description
Breeding birds, at 5–7 inches long, are grayish above and buff below with a white-rimmed tail. Autumn birds are streaky gray-brown above and heavily streaked white below. The thin legs and beak are dark.

Preferred Habitat
Males establish nesting territories on alpine or Arctic tundra before the snow melts, ready for a quick breeding

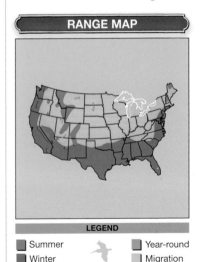

RANGE MAP

LEGEND

Summer
Winter
Year-round
Migration

gray

As the herald of spring in northern states, the robin's chipper call of *cheerily cheer up cheerio* pierces the early morning stillness. Although technically a thrush—and the only widespread thrush in America—the bird is named for its resemblance to the red-breasted robin of Europe.

Description

The male, at 9–11 inches long, is gray on top, with a black head and bright red breast. The female is similar in appearance but duller, with a gray head.

Preferred Habitat

Lawns, gardens, parks, forests, and farmland are favorite locations, but birds that winter in the northern states may roost in cedar bogs and swamps.

Feeding Habits

As it hops across a lawn with its head cocked, the robin is hunting for insects and earthworms. Berries provide sustenance through the winter.

Migration Habits

Though not all robins head south for the winter, each year huge flocks of up to 300,000 birds head northward in spring, with each bird returning to the area of his birth.

Placement of Feeders

While not regular visitors to feeders, they may be drawn to mealworms, bread, raisins, or fruit. They are easily sighted on a grassy lawn rooting for worms, and may build nests on ledges or windowsills.

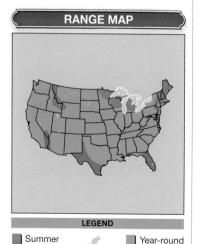

RANGE MAP

LEGEND

Summer

Winter

Year-round

Migration

gray

Feeding Habits
Garbage dumps, cemeteries, and farms are favorite hunting grounds for rodents, small mammals, or other birds. The owl has good daytime eyesight, but can track its prey by sound alone in complete darkness.

Migration Habits
The barn owl inhabits almost all states year-round, laying eggs in buildings, hollow trees, caves, or burrows. They also practice population control, producing few or no eggs when food is scarce.

Placement of Feeders
These nocturnal hunters can be seen soaring alongside highways or rural roads at dusk as they scan the ground for prey, and they may select a local barn or bell tower for nesting.

Piercing the night with a spine-tingling hiss and scream, the barn owl pursues an evening meal of mice or rabbits. This owl species is tolerant of human presence, often making its home in barns.

Description
The barn owl, at 13–19 inches long, is easily recognized by its long legs, dark eyes, and heart-shaped face. Colored golden brown with a greyish hue above and white below, it appears pure white in flight.

Preferred Habitat
A widespread species, the barn owl is found on six of seven continents, where it inhabits grasslands, marshes, deserts, and residential and urban areas.

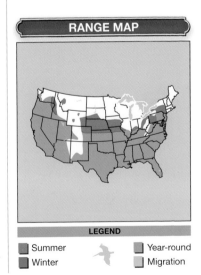

RANGE MAP

LEGEND

- Summer
- Winter
- Year-round
- Migration

A long a quiet river bank, a large blue-gray bird with a ragged crest issues a rattling *crick-crick-crick* from a nearby perch. The kingfisher is an aggressive, independent hunter.

Description

Pigeon-sized at 11–14 inches long, this crested bird is blue-gray above with a crest and white collar. The male has a blue-gray band across the chest, while the female has two chest bands and brighter coloring.

Preferred Habitat

These fish-eaters never stray far from water. The mating pair tunnels into the bank alongside a favorite river or lake, where the female lays eggs in the cool, dark burrow.

Feeding Habits

Hovering over the water, a flash of blue spirals into a deadly dive, clutching a stunned fish back to its perch, where it beats the fish and swallows it whole. Bones and scales are later regurgitated as pellets. Favorite foods include fish, tadpoles, salamanders, frogs, insects, crabs, or crayfish. Young are taught to retrieve dead fish from the water.

Migration Habits

Found year-round throughout the South, this fierce fisher travels to northern border states during summer only.

Placement of Feeders

Patient observation along the water's edge will reveal favorite perches and may allow you to witness their diving spectacle.

RANGE MAP

LEGEND

- Summer
- Winter
- Year-round
- Migration

gray

Feeding Habits

Insects, especially agricultural pests, make up about half of the chickadee's diet, supplemented by berries and seeds from shrubs, pines, and weeds. Usually traveling in pairs or small groups, chickadees swiftly communicate each flock member's successful foraging location or strategy.

Migration Habits

In the Southeast these birds are a common permanent resident from Texas to New Jersey. In autumn, they join up with mixed flocks of kinglets, creepers, warblers, titmice, and nuthatches.

Placement of Feeders

Backyards with sufficient trees and shrubbery are often host to the cheery chickadee, who readily visits seed feeders with its mixed flock.

This perky species is very similar to the black-capped chickadee, but their ranges replace each other geographically. Its four-syllable *phee-bee, phee-bay* whistle is twice as long as the black-cap's song.

Description

At only 4.5 inches the Carolina chickadee is one of the smallest in its family. The handsome bird is gray above and pale buff below, with a black cap and bib, and white cheeks.

Preferred Habitat

These chickadees are woodland birds, residing in deciduous, mixed, and coniferous forest, wooded swamps, gardens, and parks. In a tree cavity or birdhouse the chickadee crafts a cup-shaped nest of moss, plants, and feathers.

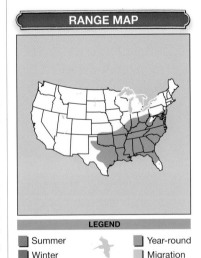

RANGE MAP

LEGEND

- Summer
- Winter
- Year-round
- Migration

gray

The dark-eyed species consolidates what were formerly thought to be up to five different species: the slate-colored, Oregon, white-winged, pink-sided, and gray-headed juncos. But despite their varied coloring, these birds breed freely with each other, and all issue a similar, slow, musical trill.

Description

All measuring 5–6.5 inches long, with a pinkish bill and dark eyes, there are distinct plumage variations. The eastern slate bird is gray above and below; the gray-head of the southern Rockies is rust or brown above; the pink-sided junco of the Central Rockies has pinkish marks on its sides; the Oregon variety has a black head and brown back, while the white-winged version of the Black Hills has white wing bars and tail.

RANGE MAP

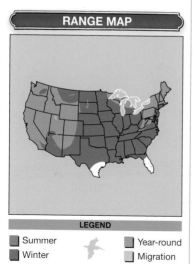

LEGEND

- ■ Summer
- ■ Winter
- ■ Year-round
- ■ Migration

Preferred Habitat

Juncos live in open woodlands and clearings throughout North America.

Feeding Habits

With a unique double-scratching motion, juncos dig for insects. They also enjoy seeds and berries.

Migration Habits

Found throughout the continental United States in the winter and migrating north in summer, the junco nests on the ground and maintains a rigid flock hierarchy. It can be found year-round throughout the western third of the United States.

Placement of Feeders

This most frequent feeder visitor prefers millet, sunflower hearts, and finely cracked corn from low platform feeders.

gray

Feeding Habits

Hunting at night on silent wings, the owl scoops up rodents, birds, earthworms, and snakes with its deadly talons. It can also catch insects on the wing or plunge into streams to snatch fish.

Migration Habits

The Eastern screech owl is a year-round resident east of the South, but on rare occasion has been spotted as far west as the mountains of Montana.

Placement of Feeders

Birders may never detect the owl's nighttime visits to backyard birdbaths, but the elusive guest sometimes uses nest boxes. Listen for their loud horsewhinny calls after dark.

T wo distinct colorings define this small owl—rusty red or mottled gray-brown. Unaffected by season, sex, or age, each bird's permanent coloring varies by relative population in a given habitat.

Description

Identified by its distinctive ear tufts, fixed yellow eyes, and white wing spots, the 10-inch red or gray owl gives a variety of chilling calls, including screeching, purring, trilling, and a descending wail.

gray

Preferred Habitat

The eastern species prefers mature deciduous forest, lakeshores, orchards, or open forest, as well as suburban areas. The female lays eggs in a tree—especially small red cedars—or nest box.

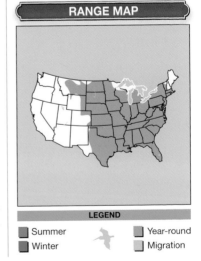

RANGE MAP

LEGEND

Summer · Year-round
Winter · Migration

Second only to the mockingbird for its impressive mimicry, the male catbird, with a special ability to sing two notes at once, fills the air with a medley of area birdcalls, shrieks, whistles, and its notorious cat-like whine.

Description

Long and thin, the catbird measures 8–9.75 inches, colored dark gray above with a black cap, and a dark rust patch on its rump.

Preferred Habitat

The catbird is at home in thickets, brush, and gardens, where it raises two broods each season in a tangle of vines or shrubs. Though tolerant of certain species, the gray catbird is territorial and may pierce the eggs of other songbirds, including cowbird eggs found in its own nest.

Feeding Habits

Ants, beetles, moths, grasshoppers, dragonflies, and spiders are found by foraging on the ground and in shrubs, while berries of the dogwood, mulberry, elderberry, and wild grape trees round out the catbird's diet.

Migration Habits

In summer, the catbird breeds across most of the continent, while it winters in the Carolinas and southward. These nighttime migrators often collide with aerial antennae and TV towers.

Placement of Feeders

This boisterous garden visitor may take up residence in a tangle of shrubs or briars alongside a house and is fond of birdbaths.

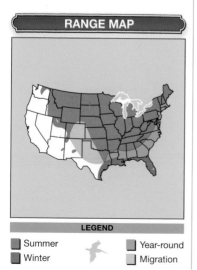

RANGE MAP

LEGEND

■ Summer
■ Winter
■ Year-round
■ Migration

gray

occasionally death. In lawns, gardens, farmland, or deserts, they live on the ground, hiding in bushes as needed, but mounting a high perch to sing.

Feeding Habits
This ground feeder forages in foliage and short grass for insects, grasshoppers, spiders, and fruit.

Migration Habits
Found year-round from California to Texas to New England, mockingbirds may migrate north in summer.

Placement of Feeders
Mockingbirds are heard singing at night more than other birds in their family, and can be identified in flight by their white wing patches and extremely slow wing beats. Suet and raisins are favorites at the feeder.

From dawn to dusk and sometimes all through the night, the northern mockingbird croons a steady, rapid stream of hundreds of bird songs, interspersed with occasional barking dog and chirping cricket imitations. Its Latin name means "mimic of many tongues."

Description
This slender, gray bird measures 9–11 inches, with a long black tail bordered by white that it flicks from side to side. Both sexes flash their two white wing bars and large white side patches.

Preferred Habitat
Fiercely territorial, mockingbirds will attack crows and grackles, and even cats during breeding season. They will also attack their own reflections with enough violence to cause injury or

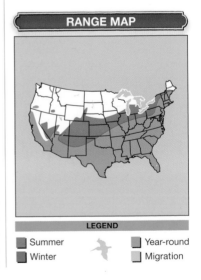

RANGE MAP

LEGEND

■ Summer
■ Winter
■ Year-round
■ Migration

gray

reeding season makes titmice anxious and irritable, and they are notorious for pulling hair from sleeping dogs, cats, and livestock to line their nests. But their cheery, ringing *peter, peter, peter!* charms at the winter feeder.

Description

Sparrow-sized at 6.5 inches, the crested bird is gray above, whitish below, with buff flanks and rusty sides. Those in Texas and Oklahoma have a black crest.

Preferred Habitat

Mating pairs seek bottomlands and wet forests, raising their brood in a hole in a mature oak tree. In autumn they roam deciduous forests with a mixed flock, frequenting gardens and parks.

Feeding Habits

Clinging to a branch, the titmouse swings upside down to pluck spiders and insects from the underside of foliage. Acorn masts and oak galls are favorites in autumn, as well as fruit and seeds.

Migration Habits

For most of the year, these birds travel in pairs, but in autumn they join with small flocks of chickadees, kinglets, and nuthatches for social foraging. From Nebraska eastward they are common year-round.

Placement of Feeders

Beechnuts, acorns, and shelled peanuts score big with these noisy, friendly backyard visitors, and mating pairs that select a nesting box on your property will stay all year.

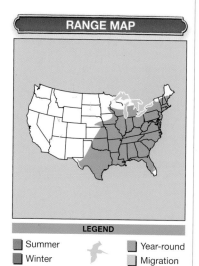

RANGE MAP

LEGEND

■ Summer
■ Winter
■ Year-round
■ Migration

gray

Feeding Habits
Using its long, thin bill, the nuthatch forages under loose bark and in tree crevices for insects and larvae.

Migration Habits
Nuthatches are found year-round in almost all continental states. Occasionally they migrate to the outer coasts in winter but are usually sedentary. In winter nuthatches join flocks of chickadees, woodpeckers, and kinglets to roam for food within their territories.

Placement of Feeders
Seed feeders and suet cakes draw these familiar winter visitors to backyard feeders. They are cheery and friendly, though not tame, and will use available nest boxes.

An extra long hind toe claw allows the nuthatch to creep down tree trunks headfirst. Like its red-breasted relative, the white-breasted nuthatch gives a low-pitched *yank-yank* call and a low whistled song, including a *whi-whi-whi-whi* mating song.

Description
Larger than the red-breast, this bird measures 5–6 inches, colored blue-gray above with a black crown and white underparts. Its black eye is conspicuous in a white face.

Preferred Habitat
Mating pairs remain together year-round, usually in dry oak or pine oak forests or other deciduous forests. Adult birds nest in a natural cavity or bird box, or excavate a new hole.

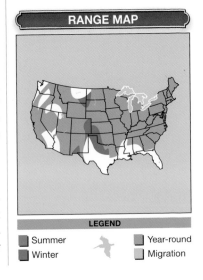

RANGE MAP

LEGEND

Summer

Winter

Year-round

Migration

white

Among white-throated sparrows, two coloring variations occur—white head stripes or tan head stripes—and birds tend to choose mating pairs with the opposite coloring. Their clear, whistled song has been transcribed in several ways, but *sweet, sweet Canada, Canada, Canada* is a common translation.

Description

The sexes look the same, measuring 6–7 inches long, streaked brown above and buff or gray below. Both have a conspicuous white throat patch, a dark bill, and yellow patches between the eyes.

Preferred Habitat

Brushy undergrowth in coniferous forests is the sparrow's preferred breeding ground, where it builds a nest of grass and moss on or near the ground under small trees. In winter, they are found in brushy

areas, pastures, bogs, and suburbs.

Feeding Habits

The sparrow captures insects by scratching on the ground, scouring vegetation, or flycatching. Weed seeds and the fruit of dogwood, sumac, and elderberry trees are also favorites.

Migration Habits

Best known in the United States as a winter visitor, they reside across most of the East and along the West Coast, with a breeding range in the North.

Placement of Feeders

In cold months, backyard bushes may be filled with roosting white-throats. They are drawn to feeders offering cracked corn or seeds.

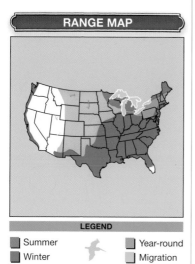

RANGE MAP

LEGEND

■ Summer
■ Winter
■ Year-round
■ Migration

white

in summer they are often found in southern deserts alongside streams.

Feeding Habits

This dove relies on cultivated fields for sorghum and other crop grains. They may travel long distances each day to reach the nearest freshwater source.

Migration Habits

Since being introduced in southern Florida, several localized populations occur along the Gulf Coast to southern Texas. In winter, they head further south to Central and South America and the American tropics.

Placement of Feeders

Watch for the white wing bands and white-tipped tail to identify this bird in the field. Cracked corn under backyard feeders may draw them into closer view.

O n a scorching hot summer day, a drawn out *hooo-hooo-ho-hooo* flows constantly from the perched dove. When startled, the dove flares from the roost flashing its bright white wing patches, clapping straight up, then soaring gracefully back down.

Description

The large, 12-inch dove is gray-brown above, and its black wings are marked with a broad white diagonal bar. In flight its white-edged rounded tail is most noticeable.

Preferred Habitat

Huge colonies of white-winged doves nest together, building fragile twig platforms in low bushes. Their preferred home is open country with dense thickets or small trees, farmland, or residential areas, but

RANGE MAP

LEGEND

Summer   Year-round
Winter   Migration

white

INDEX

INDEX